Senile Dementia

SENILE DEMENTIA? - ISN'T THAT WHEN ELDERLY CLIENTS DISAGREE WITH YOU ABOUT WHAT'S BEST FOR THEM?

Senile Dementia
Policy and services

Bernard Ineichen

Senior Research Fellow
Newham Health Authority
and The Polytechnic of East London

London   New York
CHAPMAN AND HALL

First published in 1989 by
Chapman and Hall Ltd
11 New Fetter Lane, London EC4P 4EE
Published in the USA by
Chapman and Hall
29 West 35th Street, New York NY 10001

© 1989 B. Ineichen

Printed in Great Britain by
T.J. Press (Padstow) Ltd, Padstow, Cornwall

ISBN 0 412 33790 8

British Library Cataloguing in Publication Data

Ineichen, Bernard
    Senile dementia: policy and services.
    1. Great Britain. Senile dementia victim. Care
    I. Title
    362.1'989768983'00941
    ISBN 0-412-33790-8

Library of Congress Cataloging in Publication Data

Ineichen, Bernard.
    Senile dementia : policy and services / Bernard
    Ineichen.
        p. cm.
    Bibliography: p.
    Includes index.
    ISBN 0-412-33790-8
    1. Senile dementia - Government policy -
England. 2. Senile dementia - Patients - Services
for - England. I. Title.
    [DNLM: 1. Dementia, Senile. 2. Health Policy.
3. Mental Health Services - in old age. WM 220
142s]
RC524.154 1989
DNLM/DLC   89-15844
for Library of Congress   CIP

CONTENTS

ACKNOWLEDGEMENTS

This book, and the empirical research on which it is based, arose out of the concern with services for people suffering from senile dementia, and their carers, shared by a number of workers in health and social services in and around a city in south-western England. Like the blind men examining the elephant, each was aware of only a part of the whole: each could view the problem only from the perspective of their own agency. None possessed an overall view of the service needs of dementing old people. Without good research to inform service planners, hands-on workers, no matter how good their intentions or boundless their energy, are largely working in the dark. This book makes no more than a start at giving them the material they need. It is dedicated to them, and to those all over the world who spend their working life 'caring for strangers'.

My thanks go to all of those at Chapman and Hall, especially Tim Hardwick, who have been so helpful and encouraging during the writing of this book. I include the two anonymous reviewers for their very positive comments: the work would have been poorer without them. And a special thanks to Gyles Glover and Lesley Harrison for their assistance in the preparation of the final version.

1 INTRODUCING THE SUBJECT

The concept of dementia has a history going back thousands of years. An ancient Egyptian papyrus of about 1500 B.C. contains the sentence 'The heart grows heavy, and remembers not yesterday', which may be the first written reference. The first physician to describe it convincingly was probably Aretaeus, writing in Cappodocia about 150 A.D. In the centuries which followed, the subject was almost totally ignored. Many medical authorities of ancient and classical times have little or nothing to say on the subject of old people with failing minds. In all probability, it was a rare event.

It was not until the first half of the nineteenth century that scientific interest in the mental health of old people grew substantially in Europe. Pinel, the French psychiatrist, described dementia as one kind of psychotic illness, but did not distinguish between intellectual deterioration and what would now be called mental handicap or retardation. His student, Esquirol, refined his idea without producing a precise definition of the condition. At about the same time, Prichard in England described a syndrome he called incoherence or senile dementia, characterized by recent forgetfulness while older memories are retained.

Major advances in neuropathology which have refined and clarified psychiatric diagnoses for older patients have only been achieved since that time. Indeed much of our knowledge of senile dementia has been accumulated in very recent times. Some thirty years ago, for example Roth (1955) identified five main 'psychosyndromes' in the elderly: senile dementia, arteriosclerotic dementia, acute confusional state, paraphrenia, and affective illness. A quarter of a century later, Blessed and Wilson (1982) were able to allocate 90% of the admissions to St. Nicholas Hospital, Newcastle, to one or other of these five categories. 122 of the 320 were diagnosed as senile or arteriosclerotic dementia.

The concept of dementia has itself been the subject of increasing refinement and precision in definition and diagnosis. Two important sub-types have been identified: Alzheimer's disease and multiple-infarct dementia.

Alzheimer's disease or Senile Dementia of the Alzheimer Type (SDAT), arises out of changes in the brain which are as yet poorly understood and identifiable with certainty only at post-mortem examination. This type of dementia has been named after Alois Alzheimer, who first identified these changes, in the earliest years of this century. Alzheimer's is the commonest type of identified dementia.

The second commonest type is multi-infarct dementia (MID), which follows a stroke or strokes affecting the relevant part of the brain. Like SDAT, it can be diagnosed with certainty only after death, although Jorm (1987, Ch. 8) reviews progress in using various types of tests which can suggest, if not confirm, its presence during the sufferer's lifetime. As will be shown in Chapter 2, some populations appear to reverse the general picture and exhibit more MID than SDAT.

Many dementia sufferers cannot, even after a post-mortem examination, be neatly categorized as one or the other of these sub-types. A considerable uncertain 'grey area' of dementia remains at present very poorly understood. Some elderly people develop dementia as a side-effect of known physical disease. Some of these conditions are curable.

Care of the demented person has traditionally taken place in the community: hospitalization is a fairly recent innovation. Well known literary examples show elderly demented people maintained in community care. Shakespeare's King Lear is an obvious if controversial example; perhaps the best known is the last of his Seven Ages of Man, 'Second childishness and mere oblivion, sans teeth, sans eyes, sans taste, sans everything'.

Literary and historical treatment of the seventh age of woman has been less benign, although the great majority of old people are, and probably throughout history always have been, women; elderly women losing their mental faculties are more likely to have been viewed as witches, and even today, often appear to find it harder to obtain professional help than elderly men. Yet until recently few old people lived long enough to experience senility, and literary examples among the work of the great nineteenth-century novelists are comparatively rare. Senility became a 'problem' principally when it was associated with poverty. The increasing concentration of old people in public institutions - hospitals, workhouses and asylums - made them objects of concern to legislators and politicians and easy prey for investigators (Rosen 1968).

By the late nineteenth century, treatment of the poor elderly with failing minds was increasingly harsh. In Britain, old people were no longer being burned as witches, but helpless and senile old people were beginning to clog up the workhouses: early examples of the 'Blocked Bed' phenomenon. Poor Law officers attempted to get them transferred to the County Asylums, to the disgust of their superintendents (Scull, 1979).

This discussion has been extended to the whole of the capitalist world, arguing that growing old is increasingly likely to result in mental illness not because of drift, selection or stress but because of the exclusion of the aged from labour markets because of the strangeness of the aged in capitalist societies.

> 'It is the aged's special status as strangers that, under conditions of late capitalism, makes them especially vulnerable to mental illness and social control because of their illness. The strangeness of the aged in traditional societies is largely defined in terms of their appearance and other physical properties (e.g. they are closer to death and to the beyond). They are wrinkled, stooped and slower (and perhaps sicker) than the rest of the community. Under capitalism, however, the aged's strangeness becomes total. It transcends the merely physical and enters the ideological sphere as well. By so doing, their strangeness makes them not only different but also suspicious and potentially subversive.'
>
> (Dowd, 1984, p.82-3)

Dowd does not make clear why this process should only occur in capitalist societies. It is likely that throughout the industrialized world, ageing has become difficult in a social sense, following the revolutions in manufacturing and communications. Such difficulties were much less likely to exist in small-scale, relatively unchanging, peasant or tribal societies, which preceded Western industrialization, and which are still the dominant type of society in much of today's world.

People born in the industrialized world around the turn of the last century have witnessed warfare and destruction, in their lifetime, on an unprecedented scale; and above all they have witnessed social changes affecting almost every aspect of life, taking place at an ever-increasing rate. In Margaret Mead's phrase, people born before World War Two have become 'immigrants in time' in today's world. Skills and strategies learned in youth, even in middle age, must be laid aside; living in the late twentieth century, in the developed world, means constantly facing new challenges, acting and thinking in new ways. This is especially difficult for the elderly. It is hardly surprising if old people find today's world confusing.

Senile dementia has arrived relatively late among medical diagnoses. It is unlikely ever to become a condition considered really interesting among large or influential numbers of doctors. Both of the specialisms appropriate to tackle it - psychiatry and geriatrics - are recent creations, enjoying low or at best maverick status within medicine. Private practice offers few rich pickings. Not many psychogeriatricians put up their plates in Harley Street.

The definition of dementia will be discussed in more detail in the next chapter, along with methods of diagnosis and estimates of its prevalence. Most of our present understanding comes from its identification as a medical, and specifically a psychiatric, problem. Medical science is the chief means by which dementia is defined and identified. While this provides a strong corpus of knowledge into which we can fit our understanding, it can also be something of a weakness. Discussions of dementia are sometimes hindered by the failure to distinguish between types of behaviour and clinically defined pathology.

Most recent advances have involved the approach from a medically derived disease model, taking as its starting point its definition as an illness, amenable to medical intervention, to be countered by services deployed on medical lines. Definitions reflect this. Probably the most useful, and widely accepted, definition of dementia, comes from the Royal College of Physicians' Working Party on Organic Mental Impairment of the Elderly:

> 'The acquired global impairment of higher cortical functions including memory, the capacity to solve the problems of day-to-day living, the performance of learned perceptuo-motor skills, the correct use of social skills, all aspects of language and communication, and the control of emotional reactions, in the absence of gross clouding of consciousness. The condition is often progressive though not necessarily irreversible.'
>
> (Royal College of Physicians, 1982)

Deciding precisely what constitutes this medically-defined condition remains far from easy. As Jorm (1987, p.3) points out, this definition does not tell us how much loss of intellectual abilities or memory impairment is required to produce the diagnosis. For consistency in diagnosis, practitioners need to agree on this.

Mental decline may be a long slow process, especially when low intelligence and neurotic or depressive character traits are present (Levy and Post, 1982). The difficulties of diagnosing mild dementia are compounded when subjects are of low intelligence or poor education.

Not even the most central terms used in this process are universally agreed: a questionnaire study of over 200 doctors and nurses at a large teaching hospital found considerable discordance over the precise definition of the term confusion (Simpson, 1984). Progress in agreement of the definition of dementia is set out in Chapter 2.

Non-medical discussions of dementia are relatively rare. Gubrium (1988) views it from the perspective of the relatives, pointing out that the burden of caregiving as perceived by them is influenced by many factors beside the degree of the sufferer's impairment. Gilleard (1984, p.18-20) has an extended discussion of the concept from the viewpoint of the psychologist. Reviewing the literature, he points to the broadening scope of the concept to include behavioural, affective and cognitive aspects. The word 'global' to encompass the loss of function, mentioned earlier in the Royal College of Physicians' Working Party, is crucial. What is ultimately involved, claims Gilleard, is more than a loss of function: it is eventually a loss of the person, a loss of selfhood. Relatives sometimes make this point when they speak of the dementing person as someone who is in essence 'already dead','a corpse the undertaker has forgotten to collect'. Studying dementia means considering 'what makes a person, what holds together the acts of an individual to give him or her personal integrity, consistency and ultimate value'. Summing up, Gilleard describes dementia as 'a progressive deterioration in all areas of brain function which maintain the individual's links with his present and past personal social and physical environment'.

2 MEASURING THE PROBLEM

A. Introduction

Dementia is strongly related to advanced age. The numbers of very elderly people are rising rapidly. In Britain the number of those over 65 has increased fourfold, and those over 85 sevenfold, since the beginning of this century. Official figures show that Britain now has a larger proportion of people aged over 65 than any other EEC country. The number of people over 85 is expected to double in the next 40 years. There are processes at work which suggest that the number of dementia cases will rise even faster than numbers of people surviving into their eighties. Octogenarians in previous generations may have been a 'survival elite' including very few with dementia. As more survive to a great age, they are likely to include a growing proportion of less fit people, including dementia sufferers kept alive by improved medical interventions such as antibiotic treatments.

So far these increases particularly affect richer industrialized countries with older populations. In industrialized countries with relatively youthful populations, such as Australia and Canada, future increases will be larger.

As for the Third World, the absence of epidemiology studies makes any forecast hazardous. Henderson (1986) considers that there is very little evidence of dementia, although relatively few people live to advanced years. He points out that American blacks, whose origins are West African, do develop dementia. Given increasing life expectancy, future widespread dementia in the Third World cannot be ruled out.

The scale of the problem makes the provision of appropriate care a considerable burden. As the elderly, economically unproductive sector of the population grows, a declining proportion of the population is left who are of working age. They must, among other tasks, finance and staff appropriate institutions for the elderly who need residential care. Many of these old people are demented. A majority of the institutionalized long-stay elderly patients in Finland are believed to suffer from severe dementia (Sulkava *et al.*, 1985). In the United States of America over a million people live in nursing homes. The proportion suffering from mental illness has, it has been estimated risen from over 50% to over 60% in the last decade. Most of these mentally ill people are suffering from dementia (Burns *et al.*, 1988).

The cost of caring for dementia patients in the U.S. alone has been estimated at 13.26 billion dollars (direct costs) plus 31.46 billion dollars for premature deaths, in 1985 (Huang *et al.*, 1988). However, it must be pointed out that these costs are calculated on an expectation of 4.28 million demented elderly people in the U.S., a prevalence of about 15% of the total elderly, which, as will be shown later, appears to be unduly high. The Health Advisory Service report (1982) considers that the 'rising tide' of elderly mental illness could turn into a flood which may overwhelm the entire health care system.

B. Groups at risk

Senile dementia is associated above all with advancing age. Few people under 65 develop the condition, and in such cases the diagnosis is particularly difficult to state with certainty. However, progression is often rapid for youthful sufferers and the prognosis is poor (Mortimer, 1983).

Other groups appear to be at particular risk. Sufferers from Down's Syndrome appear to dement much more frequently than would be expected by chance. The genetic nature of that condition may provide valuable clues in our understanding of some types of dementia. Close relatives of those with Down's Syndrome also have a heightened risk of developing one type of dementia, Alzheimer's Disease (SDAT) (Henderson, 1986). The nature of the genetic link in Alzheimer's disease is a matter of interest but details are still far from clear. The excessive prevalence of SDAT in first degree relatives is found more commonly in cases of early onset (Heston, 1984; Jorm, 1987).

Other groups showing vulnerability to dementia are alcohol abusers, those suffering from head injuries and most recently AIDS sufferers (Fenton, 1987). Dementia may occur in HIV disease independently of AIDS (Riccio and Thompson, 1987). AIDS may be misdiagnosed as SDAT (Weiler *et al.*, 1988).

C. Problems in measuring dementia

Dementia is often difficult to define with precision.

It is not always easy to distinguish dementia from delirium or depression. Accurate definition of mild dementia is especially difficult. Cognitive decline in the late 60s and beyond is well documented (Holzer *et al.*, 1984) but the identification of dementia sufferers from others with reduced mental ability is not easy.

'The demented patient shows changes in cognition, affect and behaviour which are hard to differentiate from those observed in normal ageing or other age-related conditions. There appears no obvious boundary between normal and abnormal ageing.' (Little *et al.*, 1987 p.808)

As Levy and Post (1982, p.169) state, where mild defects have been present over many years without marked worsening, precise differentiation between benign forgetfulness and senile dementia becomes irrelevant, especially in very old people. Poor cognitive performance may be a feature of the lives of dementing elderly people for up to 20 years prior to the onset of recognizable dementia. Poor cognitive performance may result from reasons other than dementia: for example, delirium, mental handicap, learning defects, language problems or physical illness (Holzer *et al.*, 1984). The precise timing of onset is often difficult to state.

Doubtful cases are often found to be under-privileged, unintelligent old people, who may also show neurotic symptoms. Henderson and Huppert (1984) consider 'There are no specific criteria by which its presences can be asserted; it is not itself a diagnosis, but rather a rubric for the early stages of several neuropathologically distinct disorders'. The heterogeneity of samples of diagnosed patients has made forecasting the progress of the condition hazardous (Cooper and Bickel, 1984).

A further influence is the purpose of the enquiry. Epidemiological knowledge draws on the work of the diagnostic scientist, the clinician and the service planner, and their roles and their approaches do not overlap precisely. The first seeks above all precision and accuracy when attempting to categorize the phenomena facing him. The second may sacrifice these as he tries as best he can to help the patient. The service planner enjoys the least certainty of the three, for both the 'problem' and his own response have to be tailored to the needs of the moment and (at a further cost to precision) those of the near future.

Much dementia remains hidden from all service givers: relatives may enter into a conspiracy of silence. For the service planner, future demand may be even harder to measure than present prevalence. Yet it is his task to anticipate and provide appropriately for future as well as present needs. Although, as we shall see, attempts to discover how many old people suffer from dementia have produced very varied results, some estimate of their numbers is essential if services are to be planned and provided rationally and effectively. The one thing that can be said with confidence regarding future demands on services is that, barring any breakthrough in effective treatment, they will be larger than present demands.

Distinguishing between the different types of dementia (see next section) is not easy: no hand-me-down test is available, and attempts at categorization so far have been made largely from hospital studies. Validating the clinical diagnosis of even the commonest type of dementia, Alzheimer's disease, is difficult (Henderson and Jorm, 1987).

D. Attempts to measure dementia in populations

(i) Techniques of measurement

A variety of interviews and tests have been used to establish the presence of dementia. Sometimes random methods have been used in combination, and recently computerization has been introduced. The diagnosis of the most clearly-defined of the sub-types of dementia, Alzheimer's disease, can only be performed with a degree of certainty at post-mortem examination. The measurement of mild dementia is especially problematic (Henderson and Huppert, 1984, pp.6-7).

Roth (1985) distinguished between three distinct purposes of assessment: to establish a diagnosis, to measure cognitive impairment, and to rate behaviour. Care must be taken to use the right technique to yield the desired answer: behaviour scales alone cannot measure the extent of dementia, and cognitive tests alone cannot produce a diagnosis. Forgetfulness may be due to other causes (e.g. depression) than dementia.

Diagnostic tests may be based on operational criteria or on interviews. The DSM III is an example of the first. Kay *et al.*, (1985) describe its use, but find it difficult to translate each term into actual items in the clinical examination. It also suffers from the common difficulty of such measures that changing the cut-off scores makes marked differences to apparent prevalence rates. Jorm and Henderson (1985) suggest refinements of its original form.

Jorm (1987) and Tym (1989) describe a range of possible tests and assessments. Clinical interviews may be of dubious validity unless well structured: the Geriatric Mental State is a structured example, based on the well-tried Psychiatric State Examination. Administering clinical interviews to large samples using trained psychiatrists is of course expensive, and achieving reliability on assessing milder levels of dementia is not easy. Attempts to compose scales which measure the severity of dementia have had only limited success (Kay *et al.*, 1985, Roth *et al.*, 1986).

A considerable number of scales have been devised to measure cognitive impairment. The Mini Mental State Examination, for instance, has been shown to demonstrate declining cognitive ability after about the age of 65, but the choice of a cut-off score to determine the presence of dementia must be somewhat arbitrary (Holzer *et al.*, 1984). Many subjects with low (impaired) scores had no recognisable psychiatric condition (Folstein *et al.*, 1985). There are also numerous scales to measure the degree of disordered behaviour, but care must be taken with all of these.

Little *et al.* (1987) attempted to compare the sensitivity of three scales: the Abbreviated Mental Test Score, a ten item questionnaire assessing memory for recent and remote events and orientation; Inglis Paired Associate Learning Test, a measure of verbal learning ability, and the Psychogeriatric Assessment Schedule, a semi-structured interview.

Results were disappointing: although the first and third of them gave similar overall rates of prevalence of marked cognitive decline (14% and 18% respectively) of a sample of 181 elderly people identified from GP lists, only half of those identified by either test were identified by both. Combining the tests was of little value, as a slight increase in sensitivity was achieved only at the expense of reduced specificity.

Two major attempts to achieve valid and reliable techniques for assessing dementia have been reported recently: CAMDEX and a computerized diagnosis (AGECAT) based on the GMS.

CAMDEX incorporates the three elements mentioned already as essential to characterizing the demented patient: reliable diagnosis, and measures both of cognitive decline and behaviour. It consists of an interview with a psychiatrist, a cognitive examination, a structured interview with a relative or carer, and ancillary medical enquiries. Administered to a sample of 92 elderly people, it showed encouraging levels of reliability and validity, and a good level of inter-observer reliability with a sub-sample of 40 (Roth *et al.*, 1986).

AGECAT is a computerized diagnostic procedure developed out of a large study of dementia in London and New York (Gurland *et al.*, 1983). Subsequently it has been applied to a further sample in Liverpool and can thus provide carefully controlled rates of the various mental illness, presented in the form of diagnostic clusters (Copeland *et al.*, 1987).

Given the nature of dementia, deterioration over time is a key feature of the condition (Whitehead, 1976), yet repeated investigations of the same sample is a very expensive research strategy, rarely practiced. As a result, very few studies of the incidence of dementia have been mounted, and most of the epidemiological data we have concerns prevalence.

(ii) Establishing prevalence

Prevalence is the measure of cases existing in a given population at any one time; incidence a measure of new cases appearing in a given population over a given period of time. Studies in the epidemiology of dementia have mostly been concerned with prevalence.

Attempts to establish the prevalence of dementia have been summarized by Henderson (1986) for Alzheimer's disease and Ineichen (1987). Each review a score of studies.

However, new information in this field has been growing rapidly, with several new studies published each year, and such reviews quickly become out of date. Precision in comparability is difficult to obtain, as most studies have some unique feature. Although many writers consider that studies of community samples show similar levels of moderate and severe dementia to those reported from the Newcastle studies of the early 1960s (Kay *et al.*, 1964, 1970), more recent surveys show generally lower figures.

Table 2.1 (adapted from Ineichen, 1987) sets out the findings from some thirty studies of the prevalence of dementia published since 1970. The great variety of sampling and measuring techniques accounts for the great range of findings reported.

One study is of particular importance: that of Copeland *et al.* (1987). This reports on the case of the computer- assisted diagnostic procedure described earlier in three locations: New York, London and Liverpool. Major differences are reported between the three cities. Numbers are slightly higher than appear in earlier reports (e.g. Gurland *et al.*, 1983 in New York and London) as Copeland *et al.* include all organic states in their figures, on the basis that acute organic states are seldom diagnosed in community samples. Their Liverpool sample, like some other UK samples (Bergmann *et al.*, 1979; Maule *et al.*, 1984) is drawn from GP lists, and may therefore exclude some elderly people in long-stay hospital wards.

Table 2.1 Studies in the overall prevalence of dementia

Author	Date of Publication	Country	Age range	Sample size	Overall rate(%)
Sternberg and Gawrilova	1978	USSR	60+	1020	24.6
Weissman et al.	1985	USA	65+	2588	16.1
T. Helgason	1973	Iceland	74-76	2462	11.9
Cooper and Sosna	1983	W.Germany	65+	519	11.4
Gilmore	1977	Scotland	65+	300	9.3
Kay et al.	1970	England	65+	758	8.8
Maule et al.	1984	Scotland	62-90	487	8.6
Gruer	1975	Scotland	65+	762	8.3
Copeland et al.	1987	USA	65+	445	8.3
Broe et al.	1976	Scotland	65+	808	8.1
Campbell et al.	1983	New Zealand	65+	559	7.7
Kay et al.	1985	Tasmania	70+	274	7.7
Weyerer	1983	W. Germany	65+	295	7.5
Bond	1987	Scotland	65+	4298	7.1
Sulkava et al.	1985	Finland	65+	1329	6.7
Pfeffer et al.	1987	USA	65+	817	6.2
Folstein et al.	1985	USA	65+	564	6.1
D'Alessandro et al.	1988	San Marino	67-87	488	5.9
Shibayama et al.	1986	Japan	65+	3106	5.8

Nilsson	1983	Sweden	70	404	5.2
Copeland et al.	1987	England (Liverpool)	65+	1070	5.2
Bollerup	1975	Denmark	70	619	5.0
Hasegawa et al.	1986	Japan	65+	1800	4.8
Shinfuku et al.	1984	Japan	65+	9218	4.5
Clarke et al.	1986	England	75+	1203	4.5
Persson	1980	Sweden	70	392	4.3
Copeland et al.	1987	England (London)	65+	396	4.3
Morgan et al.	1987	England	65+	1042	4.3
Bergmann et al.	1979	England	65+	800	3.1
Schoenberg et al.	1985	USA	70+	2226	3.1
Pinessi et al	1984	Italy	65+	3440	2.0

(iii) Incidence

Henderson (1986, p.5) reviews studies of incidence, which are few in number on account of the complexity and cost of necessary fieldwork. The most interesting and robust comes from the Swedish island of Lundby, whose entire population of some 2500 people was examined several times between 1947 and 1972. The resulting incidence rate for dementia is 0.7% for men and 0.5% for women in their seventies, and 1.9% for men and 2.5% for women aged 80 and above. These figures conceal the most interesting findings of all, namely that incidence rates for the second period of the study (1957-1972) are lower than for the earlier years (1947-1957) for both men and women, for all levels of severity.

There is no decrease in incidence for younger women (under the age of 80) whose disease is more likely to be affected by obvious biochemical changes, and less by environmental factors. The researchers feel that environmental improvements may be responsible for their overall findings:

'There is a great difference between being 80 years old today and 50 years ago, and there are obvious social changes from the end of the 1940s to the beginning of the 1970s. The situation for elderly people has changed for the better in many ways. This is especially true when it comes to the basic social security that has gradually been created in the Swedish society. This comparative economic security has placed elderly people in a materially improved situation, which has brought about better nutrition etc., as well as it has, above all, created possibilities for increased social activity.'

(Hagnell *et al.*, 1981, pp.208-9)

Improved physical health by for example the control of high blood pressure by hypertensive drugs, reducing the incidence of stroke, may contribute to this decrease (Bergmann and Jacoby, 1983). This suggestion receives support from a later paper by the Lundby team (Rorsman *et al.*, 1985) which shows that in the latter period of the research, dementia sufferers, like other old people, were living longer. One result of this process is that while prevalence of dementia in the latter period has fallen, the fall fails to reach statistical significance, unlike the rates for incidence reported in the earlier paper.

E. Influences on the epidemiology of dementia

(i) Age

Numerous of the studies listed in Table 2.1 illustrate the association of the rate of senile dementia and advancing age. Cognitive ability has been observed to decline from about the mid 1960s (Holzer *et al.*, 1984). Copeland *et al.* show prevalence rates of organic disorder (mainly dementia) rising from 2.1% of women aged 65-69 to 25% of women aged 85-89, and from 0.7% to 5.0% of men in these age groups (1987, Figure 1, p.819). Incidence shows similar increases, the Lundby study reporting an incidence rate for senile dementia (presumably mainly of the Alzheimer type) of 0.7% and 0.5% for men and women in their 70s, rising to 1.9% and 2.5% for those aged 80+ (Henderson, 1986).

What is less clear is whether rates go on increasing among people in their nineties. Some evidence suggests there is a plateau effect. Copeland *et al.*'s rate for the women over 90 came down to 16.7%. There are several reasons why such evidence should be treated with caution: numbers in most studies are small, survival may be selective (people who survive into their nineties may be very tough and resilient physically) or very old people with dementia die relatively more quickly in the course of the disease; and evidence from autopsy studies suggest that very old people may have a reduced risk of developing the brain lesions characteristic of Alzheimer's disease.

Given the shifting age composition of the oldest groups in the populations of the developed nations, it is clear that a single prevalence rate based on the number of over-65s is of very little use, and may actually be severely misleading (Arie, 1986; Ineichen, 1987).

(ii) Class

The relation of social class and mental illness among elderly people has been the subject of little research. Cooper (1984) notes an inverse association between mental disorder and physical disability with occupational class among elderly people. The excess of mental illness is accounted for solely by organic conditions. The rate of mental illness was especially high among people living in poor material conditions. Murphy (1982) found more depression in an East London sample, and notes the contrasting class experience of people in old age. The relationship of senile dementia and social class has been almost totally ignored. Kay *et al.* (1964, 1970) found no association, but few other writers have considered the subject. Gurland

(1981) and Weissman *et al.* (1985) found more dementia among those with less education; the difficulty of achieving precision of diagnosis among mildly demented people of low intelligence or poor education has already been noted. Holzer *et al.* (1984) found a systematic relationship between education and cognitive ability, with the highly educated not only performing better, but showing less of an age-related decline.

Other class and cultural factors than simple occupational class may influence the life-style of old people, and thus indirectly influence the prevalence of dementia. Overall levels of education and nutrition have been rising. Against this isolation may be increasing. Very large numbers of elderly people live alone, and many of them have no contact with close relatives. The effect of such social changes on the figures for dementia can only be guessed at.

(iii) Sample

One of the major influences on the figures for the prevalence on dementia shown from the studies quoted in Table 2.1 is the sampling frame used. Studies which use G.P. lists omit those in long-stay hospitals and clearly are likely to underestimate cases of severe dementia where a long-stay institution would otherwise be included. The prevalence of dementia is considerable in many types of residential institutions for the elderly: this is discussed in more detail in a later section. Small samples are more likely to be subject to experimental error (Lindesay, 1987). Few studies have been conducted in communities segregated on the basis of age: a high prevalence rate (15.3%) has been reported from a retirement community in Southern California (Pfeffer *et al.*, 1987) although excluding questionable dementias reduced this to 6.2%.

(iv) Sex

There is considerable evidence (Weyerer, 1983; Cooper, 1984; Maule *et al.*, 1984) that even controlling for the greater longevity of women, more elderly women become mentally ill than elderly men.

Dementia alone is less clear cut. Some evidence (Broe *et al.*, 1976; Helgason 1977; Campbell *et al.*, 1983; Holzer *et al.*, 1984; Bergmann, 1985; Schoenberg *et al.*, 1985) shows little or no difference between the sexes. Other surveys (Gurland *et al.*, 1983; Maule *et al.*, 1984; Pinessi *et al.*, 1984; Weissman *et al.*, 1985; Sulkava *et al.*, 1985; Clarke *et al.*, 1986; Morgan *et al.*, 1987; Copeland *et al.*, 1987) find more dementia among females. Only a handful of studies covered in Table 2.1 (Bollerup, 1975; Persson, 1980; Pfeffer *et al.*, 1987) find an excess of males. Perhaps this finding from the Scandinavian studies is influenced by the effect of alcohol, which so dominates the psychiatric scene in those countries. The retirement community studied by Pfeffer *et al.* may have considerable appeal for wives caring for dependent husbands, accounting for the excess of demented males found there.

(v) Location

Most surveys have been held in urban locations. None has been conducted with an exclusively rural sample: three (Gruer 1975, Weyerer 1983, Clarke *et al.*, 1986) have taken place in areas comprising a mixture of small towns and countryside, and those have produced very different findings.

There has been one recent major attempt to compare the prevalence of dementia in different locations: the study of mental illness among elderly people in London, Liverpool and New York conducted by Copeland and his team. In their latest paper (Copeland *et al.*, 1987) they report figures of 4.3% for London, 5.2% for Liverpool and 8.3% for New York for diagnostic syndrome cases of organic disorder which are probably mostly dementia. The prevalence for males is similar in London and Liverpool, but higher in Liverpool for females. It is difficult to know precisely why this should be so, or why the figures for New York should be so much higher than for both English cities. However, rates of mental illness for all ages in New York are considered generally to be high: one particularly thorough study of the residents of Midtown Manhattan (Srole *et al.*, 1961) found very high figures.

(vi) Ethnicity

Ethnicity as an influence on patterns of dementia has received even less attention than social class. Differential survival rates are likely when multi-ethnic populations are considered. A study from Mississippi (Schoenberg *et al.*, 1985) found that although the population of the county under consideration was split into two almost equal ethnic groups (49% black, 50% white) the population aged over 40 was 39% black, 60% white. Age-adjusted rates for severe dementia found higher prevalence rates for blacks among both men and women. However, Holzer *et al.* (1984) found little difference between racial groups in another American study, once length of education had been controlled for.

Studies of oriental populations (Henderson 1986; Hasegawa *et al.*, 1986; Serby *et al.*, 1987) have found that contrary to the general trend, they report more cases of MID than SDAT. Folstein *et al.* (1985) report a similar finding among US blacks in Baltimore.

F.   How long do dementia sufferers survive?

Gilleard (1984, Ch.1) has an extended discussion of the onset of dementia.   Most accounts rely on the recall of relatives, which is highly unreliable.   Services may be notified for reasons which do not correlate with the patient's mental decline; they may have more to do with the carer's powers of observation or ability to cope.   Longer survival times will lead to an increase in prevalence rates.

This tendency is apparent in the Lundby study, where dementia sufferers appear to be living longer; what must not be forgotten is the general increase in life-expectancy, which appeared to be improving dramatically among mentally healthy women, but not mentally healthy men (Rorsman *et al.*, 1985).

Most of the studies cf the survival time of dementia sufferers have concerned old people already in institutional care. Cooper (1987) found 42% of dementia sufferers in general hospital wards had died within a year, against 18% of other patients.   Several of the studies quoted by Gilleard report a survival rate of two years from the time of admission.   Evidence suggests this may be increasing, according to a review of longitudinal studies (Christie, 1985).   Two recent reports suggest a much higher figure might be more accurate.   Heston *et al.* (1981) used autopsy records to study SDAT patients, and Diesfeldt (1986)   reported on a sample of 297 patients in psychogeriatric nursing homes in Holland.   Each suggested an average survival time of about seven years.   There is increasing evidence that higher mortality rates are associated with early-onset; the position with late-onset cases is unclear, in view of the difficulties of establishing age of onset, and the confounding role of the physical diseases of old age.

G.   Dementia and residential care

Levels of institutionalization of elderly people vary from country to country (Grundy and Arie, 1984) and from decade to decade.   Types of   institution also vary: the increase in residential places in Britain in recent years has been almost entirely in places in voluntary or private homes. Despite an official commitment to community care, the total number of places in voluntary homes remained almost static between 1978 and 1984. The only major expansion has come within private homes, the great majority of whose residents pay their own costs (Grundy, 1987).

Epidemiological reviews (e.g. Kay and Bergmann, 1980; Henderson and Kay, 1984) note that many studies report the great majority of dementia sufferers live in the community, but this is not always the case. Several Scandinavian studies show a majority of identified dementia sufferers being in institutions (Sulkava *et al.*, 1985). Preston (1986, p. 226) has calculated that in the Australian state of Victoria, in 1981, 48% of the demented elderly were living in institutions. Although only some 6% of the elderly population were demented, almost 40% of those in institutions were. Preston attributes these differences chiefly to differences in overall institutionalization rates.

It is probable that many residents in institutional care are dementing. A majority of residents in nursing homes in America are believed to be suffering from dementia (Rabins, 1986; Burns *et al.*, 1988). A German study (Cooper, 1987) found more dementia and other mental illness among elderly people in general hospitals than would be expected in the community. Evidence suggests high rates in local authority homes in Britain. A recent study in the London borough of Camden concluded that 78% of the residents in its old people's homes suffered from dementia to some degree (Ames *et al.*, 1988). Reliable surveys in the private sector are scarce, although one study (Challis and Day, 1982) found 17% of a sample of 167 residents were reckoned to be mentally ill or confused at admission. Standards of staffing and care in residential establishments in Britain generally do not inspire confidence in the ability of such places effectively to treat mental confusion among residents.

International studies of the subject are understandably few but a comparison of old people in residential care found 16% assessed as suffering from dementia in New York and Mannheim, West Germany, and 21% in London (Mann *et al.*, 1984). In each city about 4% of elderly people were cared for in long-stay institutions, although the composition of such institutions varied; in London fewer of the beds provided essentially nursing or medical (as against other forms of residential) care, and very many more were in public, as against private, facilities, when Qcompared with provision in New York and Mannheim.

H. What will future epidemiology look like?

Many factors may influence future changes in the epidemiology of senile dementia, and their influence cannot at present be estimated.

These factors include:

* changes in the elderly population structure
* the success of treatments for organic condition
* changes in social and cultural influences on old age, such as diet, family composition and isolation, which will effect onset and subsequent development of the condition.
* the response of services, which will affect how long elderly people can be kept alive.

Large scale cohort studies of elderly people, preferably conducted simultaneously in several locations, are needed to provide baseline data, but in the present economic climate there appears little chance that such work will ever be carried out (WHO 1986).

Changes in the population structure of the elderly are taking place all over the world. In the 'already aged' countries of Europe the numbers of very old as a proportion of all elderly have been growing for a decade. In the 'newly old' developed countries, this process is just at take-off point. In the Third World, it is as yet too early to make accurate forecasts, but a 'dementia explosion' is not inconceivable.

Attempts to measure prevalence based on particular surveys in one location can be misleading if put forward as an indication of the prevalence of dementia everywhere. Where this has been tried, it is at best highly dubious and may actually be misleading. Flat-rate estimates based on the size of the population of over-65s are of little value where, as in Britain in recent years, the population structure of the elderly has been changing rapidly.

There is a danger in bandying about horrifying statistics of talking ourselves into a worse situation than exists. The statement that 'ten per cent of the people of 65 and over and 20 per cent of those over 80 show evidence of intellectual failure, that is, of dementia' (HAS, 1982 p.3) appears in the light of recent research, to be a considerable over-estimate. A rule-of-thumb of 1% of 65-74s and 10% of over 75s has been suggested as a closer approximation to the truth (Ineichen, 1987).

Yet raw numbers indicate a different prospect. Given the

likelihood of further large increases in the numbers of very old people, and the probable longer survival time of dementia sufferers, the problem is almost certain to increase from its present level. The scale of such an increase may have been severely under-estimated. The implications of this increase are obviously huge, however difficult it remains to obtain precision in attempting to measure the numbers involved.

There is at present no cure for dementia. Planning therefore for an increase in the scale, flexibility and sophistication of services to match the existing demand upon them should be at the top of the agenda for every health authority and social service department. Mobilizing and co-ordinating the response should be the concern of everyone involved from those at the centre of government to the individual caring relative.

The next chapter reviews recent developments in service provision for elderly people suffering from dementia. The remainder of the book describes research carried out to provide the basis for the planning of comprehensive care within two designated and contrasting localities.

3 RESPONDING TO DEMENTIA

Models of Health Service organization

The total needs of the severely demented old person make enormous demands on the energies of those who provide the day-to-day care. Considerable problems must be faced by those responsible for organizing formal care, in knowing how best to set about the task. The all-embracing nature of the condition's demands have been well described:

> 'Not the stuff of the analyst's couch, nor the academic clinic. It is coarse and bludgeoning in its destruction and shameless in its demand for service of the crudest, most engulfing kind. Words, medicines, sophisticated investigations are puny and often irrelevant; time, organised old-fashioned care by resourceful people in appropriate buildings are effective. Yet these are scarce, expensive and under-valued'.
>
> (Jolley, 1981, p.73)

In recent years the scale of these demands have increased due to the sheer growth of numbers of elderly people in the population. This means a growth in the numbers of those making heavy demands on health and welfare services. Hospital admission for all diagnoses rose among people over 65 by 45% between 1973 and 1983, and in those years the admissions for dementia doubled, although increase in the figures for first admissions were much more modest (Smith et al., 1986).

Growth of residential provision of all kinds has not matched the growth in numbers of elderly people. Grundy and Arie (1982, p.802) suggest age-related levels of residential provision are falling, although this trend has been partly offset by the rise in places in private residential homes (Grundy, 1987). England

and Wales have a smaller proportion of their elderly population in medical and social welfare institutions than six of the seven industrialized countries with which comparison has been made (Grundy and Arie, 1984).

At the same time that the elderly population is growing, social changes - smaller families, more brittle marriages, and the movement of population, especially young families from country to town and from decaying urban centres to suburbia - have influenced the extent of care available from relatives who might be expected to look after old people. The range of kin prepared to help is narrow, and their resources often strictly limited.

A large proportion of the response from official agencies has been to rethink and enlarge medical service provision. Initially the interest of the DHSS in the early 1970s was in response to the activities of a handful of individuals and teams in various health authorities who were planning, managing and delivering services in various innovative ways. In particular, several districts had established Joint Psychogeriatric Assessment Units as a result of the combined efforts of geriatricians, psychiatrists, and social services departments (Coleman, 1982 p.6). When these kinds of units were established more generally, however, they were not always successful, as problems arose due to the 'silting up' where services were overwhelmed and could not achieve the necessary throughput (Godber, 1978).

During the 1970s DHSS support for district old age psychiatry services grew, and the Health Advisory Service reviewed services at local level and issued annual reports. Particular individuals continued, however, to be extremely influential on the local scene, and much of the advance in services at that time was due to individual energy and enterprise. The HAS issued its timely report, *The Rising Tide*, in 1982, drawing on its accumulated wisdom, and reviewing advances made in service development in order to point the way forward.

Awareness of the need for co-ordinated planning has grown slowly. This has involved not merely a greater readiness by health authorities, local authorities and the voluntary sector to work together, but a willingness both to involve staff at all levels (bottom-up planning) and to listen to the voice of the consumer. One aspect of this movement has been the dispersal of the planning process: the introduction of what has been called 'locality planning' (King and Court, 1984).

Yet the essentially locally-stimulated nature of these changes means that innovation and the pursuit of high standards has been random and at times a hit-or-miss affair. There are strong similarities in this picture to the patchwork impression of planning by RHAs of their services for people with mental handicap (Wertheimer *et al.*, 1985). Horrocks (1986) sets out a detailed listing of the service requirements for a district's provision for elderly people, although he considers that not one DHA provides the entire range.

In practice, a more optimistic and lively atmosphere has undoubtedly been created, and a whole spectrum of service development has taken place during the 1980s. The scale of provision remains however extremely patchy. Norman (1987, Ch. 2) reviews recent progress. Variation in the scale of provision among Regional Health Authorities in hospital places, for example, range from 2894 in West Midlands to 552 in Oxford. Over 70% of NHS places continue to be provided in traditional psychiatric hospitals, and only 5% in local units. Wattis (1988a) surveyed the activities of psychogeriatricians, finding that both they and other resources were clustered in some areas more than others.

The provision of residential places in local authority homes is equally variable. Nearly half of the London boroughs, for example, reported that they made no specialist provision for demented old people (Norman, 1987).

One of the difficulties in service development has been the novelty of specialist dementia services. The principal medical specialism involved, psychogeriatrics, has grown fairly quickly, but relationships with other branches of medicine have not been without conflict. In particular there have been difficulties with adjacent medical specialities, psychiatry and geriatrics, and mutual problems have to be worked out. *The Rising Tide* (HAS, 1982 p.24) lists various options:

(i)   Psychogeriatrics within general psychiatry
(ii)   Psychogeriatrics within geriatrics
(iii)   No separate department.

The second option, a unified service for elderly sick people, appears the most constructive and may eventually be the most popular choice. Godber (1978) describes some examples from the early 1970s where the psychiatric wards were taken over and run by the geriatricians. He sees a unified provision as enhancing the status and power of the geriatric service: support for GPs will be more coherent and the attitudes of social service departments easier to influence. The question of how to separate the organic and functionally ill remains if treatment of the latter is carried out within general psychiatric units.

Not all elderly patients can be categorized neatly as 'organic' or 'functional', a problem the Joint Psychogeriatric assessment units had not completely solved. Shulman (1981) argues that those with functional illnesses need very separate treatment and different staff orientation from other elderly mentally ill patients. Both Shulman and the authors of *The Rising Tide* consider that a service providing exclusively for dementia sufferers will produce difficulties over staff morale, recruitment and work satisfaction.

Case studies are now appearing which test out the various models of organization. Perhaps the best known is the unified department of health care for the elderly in Nottingham (Norman, 1982; Arie, 1983). Among its positive effects is a greater show of interest towards working with the elderly among medical students following their placement with the department (Arie, 1984).

Jolley *et al.* (1982) describe the difficulties of developing a unified psychogeriatric team in South Manchester. Previously dementia patients had been dealt with by the geriatricians, and the need for a coherent unified service meant forging stronger links with the social service department, creating a makeshift day hospital, and stepping up domiciliary services to maintain people at home whenever possible. In the core hospital, dementia patients (and the efforts of junior doctors) were spread around several wards, as none wanted 'the image of incurability, physical dependence, non-communication and incontinence'.

Two health districts in the West Country, Worcester and Hereford, provide contrasting models. Worcester has established two specialist units of 68 and 24 beds for 'elderly severely mentally infirm', that is, patients with severe dementia but no other significant physical illness (Stilwell *et al.* 1984). In Hereford, Kyle *et al.* (1987) report the establishment, following the appointment of a new psychogeriatrician in 1977, of a Department of Mental Health of the Elderly service in Hereford District Health Authority. However, the title is something of a misnomer, as functionally ill patients are excluded, and treated by conventional adult psychiatry services. The experiences of 130 patients were recorded, 28 of them in detail; only two were found to be using services which were more expensive than long-stay residential care.

Changing professional roles

Another way to chart the extent of progress is to consider the various professional groups involved.

The number of consultant psychogeriatricians has been rising steadily for a number of years. In 1985/6 there were an estimated 250, serving some 70% of the population (Wattis 1988a). The organization and style of service they provide is varied, even idiosyncratic (Arie and Jolley, 1982). Not all of them are full-time in the speciality. This fact is not always considered disadvantageous. *The Rising Tide* (HAS, 1982, p.12) states that consultants in the psychiatry of old age should consider old-age psychiatry as their major commitment, but full-time work in this area may lead to isolation, especially if other consultants believe that one consultant's full-time commitment excludes other consultants from all work with the elderly mentally ill. The unstated message is that full-time involvement with the elderly mentally ill is a less than ideal occupation for an ambitious psychiatrist.

An alternative view gives a positive slant to psychogeriatrics: in contrast to the sometimes disappointing experience with treating younger people because of their 'inborn or early acquired personality weakness', many late life disorders occur in people who have led healthy and successful lives, and whose remaining years can be made lastingly more tolerable by timely psychiatric intervention. Post (1983, p.293) hopes psychiatrists will gradually come to realise this and will become increasingly eager to become involved with older patients.

Much still needs to be done, especially in terms of training: despite a substantial increase in the number of training posts at senior registrar level in the 1980s, they remain at only two thirds of the level within general psychiatry (Wattis, 1988b).

The response to mental illness among growing numbers of elderly people has coincided with the running down of the large psychiatric hospitals. Alternative regimes to traditional long-stay wards, and alternative residential options to the long-stay hospitals, are emerging. Often these result from the efforts of particular individuals and institutions. Whitehead, for example, has led a revolution of the elderly psychiatric service in the Brighton area. In 1966 the only in-patient facility had been at Haywards Heath, 20 miles away! Whitehead has established small psychogeriatric units and day hospitals nearer the major concentrations of elderly populations on the south coast, and has used the private sector as an adjunct to his own increasingly community-based service (Whitehead, 1983). He has refused to discriminate between long-stay and short-stay facilities, with a consequent improvement in the performance of patients who have been designated long-stay. Fewer beds are needed as patients are not kept waiting for a transfer from an assessment to a rehabilitation or long-stay ward (Whitehead, 1981).

Fraser and Healy (1986) report a successful innovation from an inner city district, where the appointment of a liaison psychiatrist assigned to mentally ill patients in acute beds in a district general hospital, succeeded in eliminating 'bed blocking' and reducing dramatically the transfer time to psychogeriatric wards. This was achieved by assisting the ward staff with treatment and discharge procedures.

Short-stay provision has proved difficult to organize with a convincing degree of success. Admissions for assessment may become jammed in hospital if the desired solution is not promptly available. This could be due to lack of appropriate provision, lack of a place in an appropriate location, or the unwillingness of relatives to receive the patient back home. However, evidence from individual units (e.g. that serving West Lothian in Scotland, described by McKechnie and Corser, 1984) suggests a better community service, and a reduction in demand for long-stay beds, may result. Short-term relief admission is designed to benefit the carer; but the patient may find the experience upsetting and disorienting, and the symptoms of dementia may increase. Allen (1983) found such costs were common among elderly people admitted to short-stay residential care.

The task of nurses has been changing too. The role of nurses on long-stay wards for dementia sufferers has always been problematic. Leff (1986) considers most of their tasks for dementing in-patients could be carried out by care assistants under nursing supervision. Norman (1982) describes some of the administrative barriers which stand between nurses and their goal of creating the best possible service for their patients. She also describes several schemes in which nursing staff have set about performing their role in innovative ways, for example by bringing reality orientation techniques onto the wards. The feasibility of attempting such changes depends, as Norman points out, not merely on adequate staffing levels but also on what activities nurses see as constituting their role. Until nursing staff redefine what they consider work, depersonalizing treatment will continue. Clearly too adequate buildings and equipment, properly maintained, are essential for good staff morale and good patient care.

Another group who have become increasingly involved with the demented elderly are clinical psychologists (Jorm, 1987; Volans, 1989). Their tasks have ranged from attempts to stem cognitive decline through techniques such as reality orientation to setting up discussion groups for caring relatives.

Innovations in residential care

Hospital and local authority residential provision have already been outlined. One alternative form of long-term care is the nursing home. Rabins (1986) considers the advantages and disadvantages of specialized nursing homes for dementia sufferers. Among the advantages:

* interested staff could be recruited
* behaviour problems reduced
* resources concentrated with training and information functions easily included
* families would approve and could be helped themselves
* cognitively intact patients would not suffer if looked after separately.

Drawbacks would be cost, the possible accelerated deterioration of the demented residents, and difficulties over deciding admission principles and overcoming resistance to entry from some potential clients and their relatives.

An alternative within the voluntary sector in Britain is that of Brendoncare (Smith, 1984). The Brendoncare foundation has created a series of residential homes, each with a nursing wing. Each resident has his or her own room possessions, and make meals in his own room. Some short-term and day care is also provided. Much of the running costs come from DHSS or NHS fees for some patients. The capital costs for construction and purchase have been raised privately. Such schemes permit patients to be cared for in the same building if and when their needs increase as their dementia (or physical illness) worsens.

Other innovations are as yet too new to be thoroughly evaluated. Norman (1987) describes over a dozen innovative examples of units providing residential care in the NHS, Social Service Departments and the voluntary sector.

Other projects mentioned briefly by Norman include the domus, a small residential unit which is neither a nursing or residential home, but will provide homely care for 12 dementing residents, with a high staff ratio. Professor Elaine Murphy plans to create up to a dozen domuses in Lewisham Health District, using a housing association as the managing agency (Norman, 1987 p.12). A recent development in Sweden (Fox, 1988) is the use of flats in ordinary blocks, staffed by nurses, which provide care for demented old people in as domestic a setting as possible. This is a health service scheme, costs being topped up by contributions from residents' pensions. Preliminary evaluation suggests that they provide an effective and positive environment (Wimo, 1988).

Another innovative type of residential care is the experimental nursing homes in High Wycombe and Liverpool which are funded by special arrangements between the DHSS and Local Health Authorities and Social Services Departments. One special feature of Highgrove House, the High Wycombe example, is its function as a teaching centre for workers in many settings who deal with demented old people. Initial reporting (Francis, 1986) suggests that it appears to be working successfully.

Those in long-stay care, however it is provided, have the same enduring needs: an individual care plan, a local service, choice and privacy and opportunity for rehabilitation (Horrocks, 1986).

Moves towards community care

Simultaneous with the growth of the new specialism of psychogeriatrics has been the movement towards community care. Community mental health centres have grown dramatically in numbers during the 1980s (Sayce, 1987). The initial effect on hospitals has been, it has been suggested, to replace those patients suffering from functional psychoses (who can now be managed in the community) with elderly dements (Godber, 1978). There is certainly some evidence that the diagnostic profile of elderly psychiatric patients has been changing, with admissions now occurring at older ages, and dementia patients surviving longer in hospital (Christie, 1982; Christie and Train, 1984).

The decline of the importance of the psychiatric hospital has meant that the newly-appointed psychogeriatricians have to be amenable to change and willing to put much of their energies to working outside the consultants' traditional locus of power, the hospital ward. The initial assessment is a case in point. There are obvious advantages in conducting initial assessments in the patient's home, and this is widely felt to be where it should always take place.

Much medical care is now given in day hospitals. Day care is now a relatively common form of service for elderly people. The 1981 General Household Survey discovered some 5% of over-65s had attended.

The development of psychogeriatric day hospitals has followed similar developments in adult psychiatry and geriatrics, although the scale of provision varies considerable around the country (Gilleard, 1984). This is especially true of services for mentally ill old people who are generally reckoned to need specialist facilities. These may provide for organic or functional illnesses only, or for all psychogeriatric conditions. Mixing organic and functionally ill patients may in practice produce difficulties of management (Norman, 1982 p.76). However a careful assessment of one psychogeriatric day hospital in Scotland, catering for both dementia and functional conditions, found such a task manageable, although overall the result could be quoted only a qualified success (Smith and Cantley, 1985).

Day hospitals may have a number of functions: assessment, short-term treatment or longer-term care, which may be necessary for reasons of medical treatment, simple care for the patient, or to give the relative a break. The last two functions may also be performed by other agencies of day care. Effective day care agencies may permit hospitalization to be delayed or even avoided altogether, or discharge to be achieved sooner.

One of the few surveys of psychogeriatric day provision was carried out by Peace (1980, 1982), who visited 27 units, which together covered a variety of functions. Most had been created at the request of the local consultant and only 18% had been purpose built. There was very great evidence of shortage of staff: 19% had no CPN cover, and there was also a great need for alternative forms of day care for those who do not need medical supervision, and transport was often inadequate. The staff's knowledge of alternative provision by social service departments or of the voluntary sector was weak. They saw maximizing their patients' functioning as their paramount task. Their hospital background, Peace (1982, p.95) feels, may lead staff to accept institutional practice as the norm.

Evaluation of these units is difficult, as there is no obvious criterion for success. Some attempts have however been made. Bergmann *et al.* (1978) found that of their sample of 83 patients, those living with children did best, those living alone did worse. For many, periods in treatment were brief. About 70% were dead or within institutional care within a year. Gilleard (1984) worked in Edinburgh where fewer than half of his sample stayed over six months. Those who did benefitted most, but shorter stays were also seen as beneficial, especially by carers. Bergmann *et al.* consider for their sample the hospitalization of some patients could have been avoided if residential care had been available earlier, a possible example of the failure of health and social services to collaborate successfully. Gilleard (1984, p.58) sums up much of the evidence about day hospitals, finding it surprisingly unconvincing, although a more recent study (Gilleard, 1987) found that day care attendance had a very positive effect on the level of stress carers report.

Patients admitted for short periods of treatment can be difficult to discharge when their conditions have improved, as they may have formed an attachment to the day hospital, or alternative forms of day care may not be available (Norman, 1982). The location of the day hospital may be important: Norman considers that premises away from hospitals may prove more suitable if they are easy to reach by patients and their carers. Certainly isolated psychiatric hospitals are unlikely to be satisfactory locations. Flexibility in providing transport can be an essential feature. This is particularly vital in rural areas: special cars or taxis may be the best solution.

A recent development has been the 'travelling day hospital' such as that described by Evans *et al.* (1986) in Hampshire, which visits four different sites each week. Most patients were referred for long-term support, through the maintenance of their skills, opportunities for social contact, and relief for carers. However, the majority of patients suffered from functional rather than organic conditions. The travelling day hospital was regarded favourably by both workers in non-health services and by patients and their families who saw it as less stigmatizing than 'the asylum'. While it led to improvements in the co-ordination and delivery of services at local level it was less successful as a focus of service development, being viewed persistently as a kind of 'hospital outpost'.

Other forms of day care provided by social service departments and the voluntary sector, have grown rapidly in numbers and importance in recent years, and these will be discussed in detail in later sections.

At the same time that important changes have been taking place in the ways hospital staff work in the treatment of dementia, other types of community health worker have been introduced.

One of the most important of these groups is the Community Psychiatric Nurse (CPN). *The Rising Tide* (HAS, 1982, Appendix II) shows almost 1500 are employed and numbers are likely to have risen in the last few years.

The creation of such a new service means that its users have initially been very varied groups. Some are hospital based, some are based in the community. The scale of their involvement with elderly clients fluctuates according to local conditions.

Lilof (1983), for instance, writes of the role of CPNs in specialized multi-disciplinary Community teams of the psychogeriatric service based on Dingleton Hospital which serves the surrounding rural areas in the Scottish borders. GPs were generally appreciative of the service especially in its ability to keep elderly patients out of hospital, although they were also critical of the availability of hospital beds. In another Scottish study, in Livingston New Town, in contrast, patients over 55 formed only 12% of the CPN workload; the commonest problem this group of CPNs dealt with were those of mood or affect of younger women (Robertson and Scott, 1985). A third Scottish study (Gilhooly, 1984) found frequent visits by a CPN associated with high morale among carers.

Experimentation and variety have become the hallmarks of CPN organization and service delivery. Nursing aides have taken over some of the CPNs' more routine tasks and 'out-of-hours' service have been developed.

Another group who have become increasingly involved are health visitors. Specialized teams have been formed in many areas. Fraser (1987) describes the work of a team of over 40 specialized 'geriatric visitors' in the London Borough of Camden, each with a caseload of 200.

Many local attempts have been made to provide regular checks on elderly patients. Verdicts on the value of this work have been varied. Early commentators (Gilleard, 1984; Fry, 1984) have been unconvinced, but more recent writers have taken a more positive stance (Harrison *et al.*, 1985; Barley, 1987). Fraser (1987) points out that the condition of many dementia patients could be improved. Murphy (1985) suggests that the groups most at risk (the over 80s, the recently bereaved, those recently discharged from hospital) can easily be identified. Community surveys to screen for dementia have found many previously undiagnosed cases.

A recent experiment using volunteers (mostly 'young elderly') was successful for one general practice in identifying elderly patients who needed referral to social or medical agencies, plus those whose needs were essentially for friendship, without creating additional work for the existing primary health care team (Beales and Hicks, 1988).

Other groups of health service workers involved in recent developments include nurses specializing in community work with the elderly (other than CPNs), nurses and others providing specialist services for the incontinent, and hospital social workers.

The tradition of district nursing is a strong one, with the advantage of ready acceptance by the great majority of elderly people. However, their organization and to an extent their role are subject to considerable variation. In the opinion of one writer, 'no two health authorities operate their community nursing services in exactly the same way' (Norman, 1982, p.26). As a result, their role in treating dementia is not always clear to define with total precision, and their relations with other groups working alongside them may be subject to friction.

Incontinence is a frequent problem, especially in the final

stages of dementia, and often appears to be the last straw which breaks the carer's will. The technology of the control of incontinence is increasingly varied. There is an argument, therefore, for a specialized service to carers on matters such as toileting regimes and the suitability of appliances.

Service responses to incontinence have been *ad hoc* and unco-ordinated. Half of all Health Districts now have a Nurse Continence Adviser (Smith, 1988). Evaluation shows a patchy performance. One such service has been successful in increasing attendance at a local clinic (McGrother *et al.*, 1986, 1987). Another (Dalziel and Richards, 1987) appeared very ineffective, stressing the need for adequate assessment and follow-up as part of a good comprehensive service.

Hospital social workers may provide a vital bridge between hospital and the community. Their role in facilitating entry, transfer and discharge from hospital and other types of residential care remains vital, especially as short-term care for assessment and the relief of carers becomes more and more common. Conventional medical social work activities like counselling relatives and looking after the welfare interests of patients are of course even more vital for dementing old people than many other categories of health service patients.

One group whose role can easily be overlooked is the general practitioners. Their service extends beyond mere medical care, embracing a vital gate-keeping function. GPs can facilitate or block contact between patients and other members of the primary health care team, and also specialist medical care and sometimes hospital beds. In view of the rising numbers of very old patients, and the growing awareness of the need to monitor costs carefully, they no longer act invariably as the advocate of the patients, but rather balance the patients' needs against the availability of services. As Cantley and Hunter (1985, p.268) put it, 'They exist not merely to distribute services among clients, but to distribute clients among services'.

The service GPs themselves provide is notoriously variable. Their training (how long ago? in what country?), their organization (single handed? group practice? health centre or private premises?) and their degree of personal interest in elderly patients may influence the service they give. Wilkin and Williams (1986) have shown huge variation exists in their consultation rates, home visits and referrals for elderly patients. According to a survey by MIND only one GP in three is interested in elderly patients or obtains any job satisfaction from this part of his work.

The catalogue of their performance is a depressing one. Various studies reveal their poor record in uncovering cases of dementia among their patients. A frequently quoted study (Williamson *et al.*, 1964) found they knew fewer than a fifth of the cases of dementia on their caseload. Gruer (1975) found psychological symptoms in 42% of a large sample of elderly people living in the Scottish Borders, including some degree of dementia in 8%. The GP had a record of these symptoms in fewer than half the cases, although 40% had seen their doctor in the past three months. Harwin (1973) found 48 of a sample of 124 physically impaired elderly people were suffering from a classified psychiatric illness, 15 of them severe dementia. The mental state of 35 of the 48 was unknown to their GP. In other studies (Parsons, 1965; Weyerer, 1983) about half the GPs' cases of dementia were missed. Gilhooly (1984) found that relatives did not always receive as much information from their GP about the patient as they expected.

These shortcomings are particularly unsatisfactory given the easy availability of simple and reliable testing tools, e.g. the Mini-Mental State Examination, which takes only a few minutes to administer and is very effective in identifying cases of delirium or dementia (Jorm, 1987).

A recent survey of seven practices in Cambridge (O'Connor *et al.*, 1988) shows GPs in a more favourable light. Pointing out that the original investigation by Williamson *et al.* identified a very high rate of dementia in its sample, O'Connor *et al.* feel that GP diagnoses may have been judged against a false standard. Their investigation found an overall prevalence of 10.7% of over 75s with dementia using CAMDEX (see Chapter 2). GP's identified 58% of these cases as demented, and 65% of those with moderate or severe dementia. However, they also considered as demented 22% of those rated non-demented by CAMDEX.

Lack of interest in the problems of the elderly appears widespread. A research report by the Surrey Council for Mental Health (quoted by Murphy, 1985) found that 38% of those who had alerted their GP to the problems of a confused elderly person reported that they were told that nothing could be done and that the symptoms were due to age. It was rare for the GP to alert domiciliary services or play any role in the co-ordination of voluntary and social services. Against this, 49% passed the problem to the psychogeriatrician without any preliminary investigations. O'Connor *et al.* (1988) also felt that GPs often recognize dementia without acting upon it. Only a third of their sample rated severely demented by CAMDEX, and a tenth of those rated less severely demented had been referred to a psychogeriatrician. In another study (Gilhooly, 1984) carers often expected the GP to volunteer information about their relative's condition, but did not receive any. O'Connor *et al.*

feel GPs (and nurses) can help relatives by encouraging them to talk about their problems.

Their poor collaboration with workers in other disciplines is confirmed by other studies.

Their relationships with social workers have been shown to be particularly lacking in effectiveness. A Scottish writer found that most GPs 'admitted that it was a mystery to them what social workers were expected to do'. They operated on different timescales, and even on a day-to-day basis found social workers difficult to contact: both groups were ill-informed about how the other spend their working day. GPs were suspicious both of social workers' image (long hair and burst tennis shoes) and their training (Bruce, 1980).

Several more recent studies show some of the limitations of the G.P. in his relation with other workers. A study of 28 GPs in rural Norfolk in 1983 found that social workers considered that many of their referrals contained inadequate or inaccurate information, but few social workers attempted to get more information from them in such cases. GPs were considered to overestimate the use of residential care for the elderly, and were generally excluded from case-management subsequent to referral (Sheppard, 1985).

Another study (Cantley and Hunter, 1985) looked at the process of decision-making by GPs. They found that GPs did not have a shared view about what constitutes a 'blocked bed' even among the local hospital beds that they controlled. Neither did they share a view about the relative priority to be attached to avoiding bed blockage. This affected the way GPs used these resources. In short, their actions were influenced by social and service considerations as well as clinical ones.

Undoubtedly some of the difficulties facing general practitioners in effectively providing their part in the care of the demented elderly people stems from the conservatism of their hospital based training. As Norman (1982, p.21) points out, few medical schools contained Departments of Geriatric Medicine until very recently. The care and treatment of old people has made little impact on the medical curriculum. Recent changes in the training of GPs giving more emphasis to periods in established practices, will certainly go some way to restoring balance, but for older trained GPs the problem remains. A recent scheme provided encouragement for them too. Jacques and Burley (1987) describe how a university department of Geriatric Medicine has introduced a series of short courses and study days which tell GPs of the existence of non-medical support agencies, apparently improving their functioning as gate-keepers and as leaders of the primary care team.

A recent study from one six-partner practice in Scotland conveys a markedly more positive impression of GP involvement. Of the practice's patients over the age of 75, 25 (3.9%) were suspected of dementia, and the diagnosis subsequently confirmed by Mental Status Questionnaire for 21 of them. The MSQ was then administered to another 50 over-75s chosen at random; none was found to be dementing, although one third showed asymptomatic mild cognitive decline. Although the authors (Philp and Young, 1988a) do not rule out the possibility that relatives denied the presence of symptoms in some cases, this practice undoubtedly presents a much better profile than those previously researched. It is noteworthy that a health visitor attached to the practice with special responsibility for elderly patients could identify all those subsequently shown to be dementing (the practice partners could each identify only a few) - although she had had no training in mental health and did not systematically test patients. This fact reinforces work done elsewhere that the attachment of a health visitor to a primary care team with specific responsibility for the elderly can result in the identification of many problems not previously known to the team (Vetter *et al.*, 1984). The Cambridge study quoted earlier (O'Connor *et al.*, 1988) underlines the value of community nurses in identifying dementia and helping the families.

Contribution of Social Service Departments

Social service provision for the elderly has had an unfortunate history. Victorian social legislation distinguished between those unable to work (e.g. the demented) and the able-bodied poor. As mentioned earlier, this led to boundary disputes between workhouses and county asylums as to responsibility for elderly mentally frail people.

Social work in the twentieth century has paid comparatively little attention to the needs of the elderly, who have been seen as a relatively unrewarding client group at a time when social work's rise has been tied to the concept of psychoanalytically-derived 'casework'. Work with the elderly has been perceived as a low status task and many of their needs have been assigned to the workload of poorly trained assistants. Recent reorganizations and consolidation of social work departments have led to a more generic service staffed by social workers who are less interested in specialization. One practical consequence has been to concentrate power in the hands of better qualified workers who have come mostly from the child-care field. The result, in words of one commentator, has been that 'skilled social work tended to be seen in terms of children and families, and the frail elderly, along with the mentally ill, the mentally handicapped and the physically disabled lost out' (Norman, 1982 p.24). Another feels that social work tasks with the elderly may not always be clearly conceptualized, and staff tend to see the needs of elderly clients in terms of services they themselves can supply (Rowlings, 1981). The emphasis on child abuse in recent years may have tipped the balance away from the elderly still further.

Social workers based in hospitals have also suffered from a downgrading in power and status within the social work profession. But the growth in numbers of dependent elderly has led relatively recently to an upsurge in interest, reflected in a growth in the numbers of specialist posts and in the insertion of courses on the elderly in social work training.

It is also led to more creative uses for field social workers, for example in the Kent community care project (Challis and Davies, 1980, 1986; Davies and Challis, 1986) where key workers can create a flexible package of care for each individual elderly client.

Alongside the field social workers, the home help service has grown in importance as a helping agency for dementing elderly people. It has found itself confronted by an increasing number of clients suffering from confusion or dementia. Home helps have two advantages in helping this client group: they spend a long time with their clients, and unlike some other workers are likely to share the cultural and social backgrounds of their working class clients. Facing this increase in their importance, the home help service has begun to seek innovation in its organization and techniques of service delivery. New initiatives are widespread. For example, Avon Social Service Department have renamed their home helps the 'Home Care Service', introduced many innovations, improved recruitment and reduced staff turnover (Dexter and Harbert, 1983).

One study of relatives of demented elderly people (Gilhooly, 1984) found that home helps were instrumental in boosting their morale and relieving their distress. Many are however allocated to demented elderly people living alone.

How to allocate their scarce resources remains a problem for management. A recent report by the DHSS Social Services Inspectorate has found that home help services were thinly spread; the majority of clients received three hours' service or less each week which has been termed the 'pebbledash approach'; home help organizers work in unsystematic fashions, with front-line workers' routines effectively determining policy; and little data on service operation was fed back to managers, to permit an effective evaluation of the service's work. Other research suggests these limitations apply widely to the efforts of Social Service Departments with their elderly clients (Hunter, 1987).

Social service departments provide day care for dependent elderly people, both in day centres and in their residential 'Part III' homes. Provision is extremely varied both in scale and quality. Carter (1981) provides an overview by means of a national survey. Much provision for day care for old people is of only marginal value for demented sufferers; for example a survey of day care in East Anglia quoted by Gilleard (1984, p.57) found only a handful of demented clients in many of the units, where their disabilities were regarded very unfavourably by other clients.

There is little evidence that day services for the demented are well co-ordinated. The study by Peace (1980, 1982) quoted earlier concerned 27 day hospitals, half of which did not know what day care provision was being made by other agencies. Services are not always altered effectively to ensure the right clients reach them: Carter found home visits by day centre staff prior to clients starting day care were very uncommon, although this was what psychogeriatricians preferred.

Again, there are signs of hope in recent years. Some isolated examples suggest a growing willingness to face up to organizational problems, and to innovate. King and Court (1984) describe a day centre run jointly by local authority and health staff (a particularly valuable initiative in rural areas, where resources must be spread thinly, and clients face long journeys to attend); and Doyle and Hunt (1985) describes a day centre run by a CPN.

Probably the most important element of social service assistance for elderly people is the provision of residential care. This stems from Part III of the 1948 National Assistance Act, which obliged local authorities to provide residential care for dependent old people. The location of many in former workhouses has given them a reputation similar to that of the old asylums mentioned earlier.

The extent and manner in which they discharged their obligation has been a matter of continual controversy. In particular, the question of how best to deal with dementing residents has never been fully resolved. How much supporting medical and psychiatric back-up is available appears very variable. One consultant (Godber, 1987) reckons to visit about ten homes a week.

'This can obviously be time consuming, but with two or three hundred (residents who are known to the service) it pays ample dividends in reducing the pressure on our beds. It also gives us forewarning of those heading towards our long-stay beds. The regular contact and advice seems also to help standards and morale in the homes.'

There is no doubt that Part III homes contain many residents who are suffering from symptoms of confusion and dementia. Investigations in the London Borough of Camden (Mann *et al.*, 1984; Ames *et al.*, 1988) have found that between two-thirds and three-quarters have been suffering from dementia of some degree of severity. In the latter enquiry only one resident in seven was totally free of the symptoms of mental illness.

Other surveys have shown rather lower figures for mental illness among residents, but considerable levels of dependency remain. Stilwell *et al.* (1984) note the growth in Worcester between 1976 and 1981 of substantial numbers of Part III residents who are not only demented but present heavy nursing demands.

The problem of whether to integrate or segregate demented residents remains. One influential contribution to this debate has been the book published by Michael Meacher, *Taken for a Ride* (1972). This gives an unfavourable view of homes which are segregated exclusively for demented residents. Norman (1987, p.5) is a recent critic of this work and worth quoting at length:

'The research appears to have been done in 1967 when there was little in the way of general awareness of the complex aetiology of confusional symptoms, and assessment techniques were in their infancy. It looked at three specialist homes in which confused old people were the majority or substantial minority and which were chosen from a list supplied by the Ministry of Health. One was a large isolated manor house with minimal modern facilities, run by a voluntary agency; one was a modern purpose-built local authority Part III home with an open-plan design; and one was the new wing of an old workhouse. All catered for a very wide mix of mental disability (one-fifth of the residents in one of the homes were classified as subnormal) and they evidently included what would now be considered a disastrously high percentage of people who get there by misadventure or lack of alternative placement.

'Meacher's methodology was based on interviews with residents, watching daily routine and the use of a 'confusion scale' devised by himself. His arguments rest on the assumption that separatist regimes *inevitably* generate the practices he observed, such as dumping people into care without discussion or explanation (being 'taken for a ride'); infantilizing procedures; heavy sedation; physical restraints; ritualized questions; and 'similar devices'. Thus Meacher's book is a pioneer in the use of observation as a research tool and is a mine of awful examples of bad practice, but it does not provide the foundation for any attack on the sort of specialist care described in this study.'

Norman goes on herself (pp.16-20) to present a national study of the extent of integration and segregation. It remains a live issue for local authorities, and the variety of solutions reflects the lack of clear agreement. Other factors such as staff ratio and management style may have a greater influence on resident satisfaction than the proportion of residents who are demented. Residents themselves do not appear unduly disturbed by fellow residents who are confused (Wilkin and Hughes, 1987). Recent commentators (Jorm, 1987; Sinclair, 1988) suggest that disturbed behaviour creates more difficulties than confusion or dementia.

Segregated facilities can find themselves facing a formidable task. Mushet (1985) notes that residents in Cleveland resemble, in levels of disability, patients in long-stay psychogeriatric wards. The staff ratio is not so favourable and staff are minimally trained. In such circumstances, caring for severely disturbed residents who may be awaiting transfer to a hospital ward can be particularly irksome. Mushet asks if one is really creating a hospital in disguise, and on the cheap.

Role of the voluntary sector

The role of the voluntary sector and the growing influence of private developments is obviously considerable, although extremely difficult to measure in detail.

The growth in private residential care for elderly people in nursing and residential care has been dramatic, but there seems little doubt that the standard of care offered to dementing elderly residents is variable.

The scale of the problem is huge. Development in Britain is variable: one county has 7000 places, another none (*The Rising Tide*, p.21). What little work that has been done on the subject suggests there is a considerable amount of dementia among the residents in private homes, with little appropriate provision to help (Stilwell *et al.*, 1984).

Other recent developments have provided marked but often uneven increases in choice for help available from the mushrooming of voluntary organizations designed to help elderly people and their carers. For example, with the help of an outside-funded paid organizer, the number of centres providing day care for the elderly mentally infirm in Buckinghamshire has risen from one to about a dozen between the early 1970s and 1982 (Simons, 1982). Collaboration in such circumstances is essential, if the best use of resoures is to be achieved. Providing for as many demented people as possible is one aim of such innovation, but this also calls for flexibility in providing a geographical spread of centres, and a wide range of types of day care for different categories of client.

A number of innovative local schemes for dealing with dementia have been created recently, cutting across agency boundaries. Among the forerunners of such schemes were those designed to provide flexible packages of care for all dependent elderly people, for example those in Kent already described. Other more specialized schemes for dependent elderly people have also been influential, such as those described by Power and Kelly (1981) using volunteers to provide long-term support by helping with simple tasks at home, and Leat (1983) providing short-term placements with families in various locations.

Recent schemes providing specifically for dementia sufferers include those described by Crosby *et al.* (1984) in Liverpool, Henneman *et al.* (1987) in Exeter, and Askham *et al.* (1987) in Newham and Ipswich. The key features of these schemes was the introduction of relatively untrained aides to provide flexible packages of support in sufferers' own homes.

A small scheme set up by the Home Care Service in Birmingham provided assistance (usually 3 or 4 hour-long visits per day by home care assistants) to 15 extremely demented and dependent clients, most of whom lived alone. Co-ordination with other services was good, and only two clients deteriorated to the point they could not be supported at home. Although demand on residential and other care services was reduced, the scheme was brought to a halt after two years on the grounds of cost (McPherson, 1987).

Another small scheme in Southampton (Rosenvinge *et al.*, 1986) cost less than one hospital bed place to run. A part-time psychiatric nursing officer trained a team of people who acted as sitters for elderly dementia sufferers, to give their carers a break. Although the number of sitters was small, the demand for long-stay beds was reduced by two places: the scheme paid for itself twice over! The Crossroads Care Attendant Scheme, and the National Council for Carers and their Elderly Dependents run their own sitting services in numerous areas, providing respite for those caring for demented or non-demented relatives. Other hopeful signs are the reporting of successful working of multidisciplinary teams from the Scottish borders (Lilof, 1983), Leicestershire (Lodge, 1986) and Coventry (La Fontaine, 1987). Conflict with primary care teams is one pitfall they must avoid (Murphy, 1985). But not all such schemes are successful; May *et al.* (1986) describe a Scottish example which collapsed.

There are also several examples of national voluntary organizations which concern themselves with dementia sufferers and their problems. Some of these, such as Age Concern and Help the Aged, provide services and act as pressure groups and information clearing houses, for the whole spectrum of elderly care. The Centre for Policy on Ageing provides an intellectual forum for the discussion of the whole range of issues concerning elderly people. The Foundation for Age Research raises funds and commissions research on the health of elderly people.

The Alzheimer's Disease Society acts as a mouthpiece for dementia sufferers and their relatives. It promotes their interests and welfare nationally, and through the operation of local groups and activity, as a co-ordinator of information and advice on dementia (it publishes an advice booklet for carers, for instance), as a pressure group, a consciousness raiser, and an investigator and innovator in local services.

In Scotland an alliance of some two dozen statutory and voluntary organizations, Scottish Action on Dementia, has been formed to campaign for better services for dementia sufferers and their relatives, sponsored by the Mental Health Foundation and Age Concern Scotland. Their first major conference provided a platform for an array of innovative service developments (Hunter *et al.*, 1987).

Other local groups have been formed throughout the country to raise funds or promote services for dementia sufferers, often through the efforts of ex-carers who have become aware of the limitations of local services, and realized how effective energetic individuals can be at mobilizing local resources.

The smallest institution of all which has been found to be useful in the management of dementia is the mutual support group of relatives and carers, often formed at the instigation of and gently directed by professional workers.

One group for instance, had a greater knowledge of dementia, felt less burdened, and were less depressed after eight weekly meetings than were those on the waiting list (Kahan *et al.*, 1985). A course for 36 carers in Eastbourne had equally positive results, assisting carers to understand the problems, learn about the practical aspects of caring, and adding to their confidence (Leng, 1987). Another function of such groups can be in helping carers, whose social life has atrophied over a long period dedicated to caring for their dementing relative or friend, by enabling them to learn to enjoy themselves again. This happened in a group in Seaford described by Rice (1984). An extreme example is quoted by Barnes *et al.* (1981, p.82): a wife who stayed with the dementing husband even when he was admitted to hospital.

'Later she realised that it would have been more reasonable to have taken a much needed vacation, but she had become so used to the idea that her husband could not get along without her that she stayed with him even in the hospital.'

Sometimes relative support groups develop to produce the nucleus of more ambitions schemes. Moore (1985) describes how a support group developed into a sitting service on the lines of some of those described earlier. At the very least the growing awareness of their position should lead carers into more corporate action designed to increase public awareness of dementia and to a greater degree of collaboration between voluntary and statutory services.

The impact on families

Much dementia remains outside the service net. Shortfalls in the knowledge of dementia sufferers among those involved in primary health care have been illustrated earlier. Gilleard (1984, p.15) suggests that there often appears to be a gap of two to three years between relatives suspecting all is not well, and their seeking the help of a doctor. Levin *et al.* (1983) who interviewed a sample of 150 dementia sufferers and their carers, in three different areas, over a period of a year, found an alarming gap between these needs and what the services were actually providing.

This lack of involvement may stem in part from the unwillingness or inability of carers to accept that their relative is mentally ill. Only 2% of a large sample interviewed on the subject considered old age as one of the main causes of mental illness; possibly the lay tendency is to see the decline into senility as a natural development rather than an illness (MORI, 1979, p.18). Another reason may be that relatives and sufferers perceive dementia as stigmatizing, and keep the problem to themselves. O'Connor *et al.* (1988) feel that relatives may not ask for help until they are at the limit of their endurance, adopting a fatalistic approach, as they think little can be done to help.

In practice the burden of caring for demented old people falls on very few people beyond the community services and immediate relatives. In Black's (1985) sample 66% had care from a single relative; friends and other relatives were mentioned only rarely. The range of relatives who care is narrow: 85% of Levin *et al.*'s (1983) sample of carers were spouses or children. They were also elderly (average age 61) and long-established, having shared a household with the sufferer for an average of 36 years. Levin *et al.*'s sample were also in less than robust health themselves: only a third rated their own health as good in the previous year, a third had symptoms of stress suggesting a need for psychiatric attention, and about a half had activity-limiting disabilities. This situation is in marked contrast with so many traditional or tribal societies from around the world described by anthropologists, where care of the dependent elderly is a routine task for the extended family.

Numerous investigations have been made into what behaviour carers find particularly difficult to handle (Gilleard, 1984; George and Gwyther, 1986; Jorm, 1987). Restlessness, nocturnal wandering, incontinence, communication problems and aggression come near the top of most researchers' lists. However, what is especially difficult for carers to cope with is the change in their relationship with the sufferer which accompanies the final stages of a dementing illness (Gilhooly, 1986). Relatives of some demented patients have been urged to become more assertive in order to manage the patient's difficult behaviour (Bergmann *et al.*, 1984).

It has frequently been pointed out that the burden of care-giving, as perceived by the carer, does not vary directly with the patient's impairment. Gubrium (1988) identifies four influences: hearing about the circumstances of others (e.g. in a support group) influences self-perception; network of kin are not always seen as supportive, and some relatives may be praised for 'keeping clear'; the family histories of the sufferer may affect how he or she is treated; and caring is carried on in the context of other family relationships, so that for example caring daughters may also have obligations to their own husbands and children.

The psychological costs of caring are marked. Most studies have shown that the carers of demented elderly people are under considerable stress (Eagles *et al.*, 1987a; Whittick, 1988) although this does not inevitably lead to mental illness. The finding may result in part from the fact that most sample studies have been assembled from referrals to the psychiatric service (Eagles *et al.*, 1987b). Several researchers have found that carers' mental health improves when their demented charge attends day care (Gilleard, 1987) and is admitted to residential care (Gilleard, 1987; Sinclair, 1988).

Carers run the risk of pejorative labels whatever they do, in the same manner as has been pointed out in the case of parents of a mentally handicapped child: hiding the problem is 'over-protection', doing nothing is 'denial' and seeking institutional care is 'rejection'. Clearly too, the day-to-day tasks of caring, and the fear of the stigma of dementia, can produce isolation of carers which confines them to their homes and can be almost all-embracing. Carers can find themselves trapped in a cycle of resentment and guilt. The stability of the marriages of the present oldest generation can become double edged:

'Present-day couples who have lived together for forty or fifty years have shared a great deal. The recent generation have gone through two world wars, seen hunger marches, a revolution in transport from horses and carriages to space travel and now accept television as a day-to-day presence when their childhood could not have dreamed of such a thing. Even when a marriage has been firmly bedded in hatred, such lengthy familiarity usually carries with it a preparedness to care for the other in disability.'

(Jolley, 1981, p.78)

One of Barnes *et al.*'s (1981) informants puts the dilemma into a graphic phrase: the demands of caring for his wife had become so great he had become 'a prisoner of love'. A further difficulty faced by those who married in the interwar period is the very segregated role pattern within such relationships: spouses find themselves in their eighties forced for the first time to perform tasks which have traditionally been their partner's. Husbands must learn cooking and housework, wives the management of finances.

Problems facing children who are carers are probably rather less intense but may be felt to be more enduring: as Jolley (1981, p.80) puts it: 'To the child the persistent presence of a slightly drab, slow, aspontaneous yet proud parent produces a drag on the natural flow of living'. The effect of the presence of the demented elder on other family members (such as grandchildren) is almost totally uncharted. Few family houses are large enough to prevent the presence of a dementing elderly relative from inhibiting the domestic lives of other family members. Gilleard (1985) found that children were less likely than spouses to make the caring role an all-embracing one.

Undoubtedly the nature of the burden of care changes over time. Gilleard (1984) notes the initial feeling of uncertainty, and the hesitant identification of what is not as it should be; the increasing need for the carer to supervise their relative's action; finally the deterioration in personal habits and hygiene, and the loss of personhood, so that the task becomes what is sometimes referred to as 'caring for a stranger'.

Black (1985) found early and middle stage dementia presented more problems than the final stage, when the sufferer became less active. Assistance may be more readily available to male carers, as men find it easier to 'share' care with service-givers. While grown-up children caring for their elderly parent may respond distancing themselves or sharing the burden of caring, spouses may give care-giving priority over other roles. Carers may find it less of a strain if they are emotionally close to the sufferer.

Demented old people living on their own present particular difficulties to services. In a study of referrals to a psychiatric day assessment unit, Bergmann *et al.* (1978) found that people living on their own had received significantly more local authority support than those living with relatives prior to assessment, but this did not appear to enhance chances of survival. Thus although family members do as the state a service by keeping their demented relative out of residential care, they receive less service assistance than is given to demented people living alone.

Few attempts have been made to provide controlled assistance to carers, and measure its effectiveness. One recent attempt (Philp and Young, 1988b) has been reported from Scotland, from one practice with a specialist health visitor attached. Providing factual information on dementia and the extent of local available services to a small sample of carers had positive results: a decrease in the stress level of carers and a decrease in the reporting of unmet needs, although somewhat paradoxically there was little change in the number of resources actually used.

4 IDENTIFYING THE ISSUES

The recent developments in service provision outlined in the last chapter point up a number of questions which face those currently involved in planning and managing services for dementing old people.

*What is the present and anticipated future demand upon services? How many people will dement, and how many of them come to the attention of the services? Should the services encourage all of them to seek help?

*What model of service organization provides the best means of delivering effective health care to this particular patient group: psychogeriatricians as a branch of the psychiatric or geriatric services? Is dementia separate from or together with other mental illnesses of the elderly? What is the role of the consultant psychogeriatrician? CPNs? How should assessments be handled?

*How can effective collaboration between health and social services best be achieved, in providing sufficient numbers and variety in residential and day care?

*How can domiciliary care be improved, so that the skills and efforts of GPs, nurses, social workers and home helps be most effectively deployed?

*Should Part III homes and private residential homes seek to integrate or segregate demented residents?

*What are the educational and training needs of staff in the various agencies and establishments that care for demented old people?

*Are staff from a wide range of agencies involved in planning towards a more comprehensive service?

*How can the energies of the voluntary sector best be mobilized and most effectively integrated with the statutory services?

*How can relatives best be helped to go on caring effectively, and their contribution channelled into positive forms of collaboration?

In the course of 1983 a group of service planners and professionals in a district health authority in South-West England, and in two of the social service departments serving the same population, came together in a series of meetings to discuss their growing concern for people suffering from senile dementia. The group comprised three consultants (two psychogeriatricians and a geriatrician), a psychologist, a nurse manager, a health service administrator, two social service managers, and a representative from a voluntary society. All were concerned for the following reasons:

*The number of sufferers appears to be growing

*Services were poorly co-ordinated

*Little in the way of coherent planning was going on

*There were no obvious channels of communication between agencies

*There was no mechanism for publishing examples of good practice in service management and delivery.

They agreed on the need for a programme of research and obtained joint finance funding to employ a researcher. In the event four projects were carried through:

1. A collation of examples of good practice: a 'Library of Good Ideas'.

2. An estimate from existing population projections, and literature on the epidemiology of senile dementia, of the likely increases in the numbers of dementia sufferers within the Health District up to the end of this century.

3. An enquiry based on interviews with 85 local service planners, managers and practitioners of perceptions of gaps and shortcomings in local services for dementia sufferers.

4. A survey of the 'careers' of a sample of 100 dementia sufferers through tracing their contacts with various service agencies over a period of four months.

The third and fourth of these exercises form the substance of the next two chapters. The research was focused in two locations: a city of 100,000, and a small town of 30,000 with its surrounding villages. Both came within the boundaries of the same health authority, but were served by different Social Service Departments. Some of the differences in service organization in the two areas are shown in Figure 4.1. The choice of two such contrasting geographical areas was particularly appropriate: *The Rising Tide* (HAS, 1982, p.22) considered that the division between town and country was the most important division affecting service organization.

Both the enquiry into service providers' perceptions, and that based on 100 cases, drew heavily on the collaboration of two general practices, one in each location. Again there were major differences between them, and these are set out in Figure 4.2.

By national standards, both areas were relatively affluent. One feature of service provision which may have been a consequence of this was the size of the contribution made to the care of dependent elderly people by private residential sector.

Figure 4.1 Characteristics of study areas

	City	Town
Health service for dementia	Separate from adult psychiatry	Part of EMI service
Location of consultant	In main hospitals	Spends much time in scattered O/P clinics
Location of geriatric wards	In geriatric hospitals	In psychiatric hospital, and community hospitals in small towns
CPN service	Separate, well developed	Still developing
Home care service	Available with little restriction to those in greatest need	Some potential clients excluded on financial grounds
Home aides	Available	Not available
Part III Homes	Specialised Part III Home for demented clients	No specialised Part III homes
GP hospital beds	None available	Available
Specialised voluntary day centre for dementia	Available 4 days a week	Not available

Figure 4.2 The practices compared

	City	Town
Location	Purpose-built health centre	Private premises shared by partners
Patient lists	No separate lists	Separate lists
Trainee	Trainee included	No trainee
HVs and DNs	Relate to health centre	Relate to particular GP
Social Worker	Attached	Not attached
Meetings	Regular, involving all care staff, including discussions of individual patients	Involve doctors only; deal largely with administrative matters
Information	Age/sex register	Age/sex register for one GP only
Gender of staff	Some doctors male, some female. Administrator male, all other staff female	All doctors male, all other staff female
Mode of address	Christian name	Title and surname

5 LISTENING TO THE PROFESSIONALS

1. The sample

Interviews were held with 85 people involved in service planning and delivery for people with senile dementia. These included 56 people with jobs of managerial responsibilities and front-line workers such as CPNs, in the health service: 15 managers and practitioners in the two social service departments; and 14 others with a local or national interest and expertise in dementia services. 21 were doctors, 29 nurses, 17 social workers and 18 from other professional backgrounds. Only one person refused to be interviewed.

The consultant psychogeriatrician, and several of his staff, were interviewed in each location. Also included were two entire primary health care teams, 24 people in all, whose features were described in the previous chapter.

2. The interviews

Interviews were loosely structured and covered the following topics.

1. Referrals: method of referral, eligibility, number on current caseload.

2. Task: organization of work in the agency, specific tasks of interviewee, tasks of other workers; when to close a case.

3. Unmet demand: waiting lists and their management: late referrals; unmet demand; benefits of earlier referral; do clients get all the help they need?

4. Relations with other agencies. Their shortcomings. Gaps in the service net.

3. The views expressed

3.1 Domiciliary services

The first category of service provision to be considered is that of the domiciliary services: those workers who provide a service by going into clients' homes. This group is of crucial importance in implementing the recent innovations in attempting to provide the help necessary to let dementing old people stay in their homes for as long as possible, as this is felt to reflect the clients' views, and reduce demand on expensive residential services.

As mentioned earlier, domiciliary workers were well represented in the interviewed sample, which contained two entire primary health care teams, and several social service staff involved in providing domiciliary care.

Four problem areas were identified in the delivery of primary care: the slowness of response of referrals, especially by local authority social workers; the variable response of the primary health care team; the problems created by fit dementing old people; the restriction of some backup services to office hours only.

3.1.1 Slowness of response to referrals

Slowness of response was a criticism raised by a variety of informants in both locations. It was levelled primarily at social services personnel. For example, a district nurse said of them:

> 'They are not fast enough. They
> don't do things today but "In a
> couple of weeks". For example, if
> bed blocks are needed, 1. the OT
> makes a visit to assess, 2. the OT
> and the technician make a visit to
> measure, and 3. delivery. They
> don't seem to share our urgency.
> The time lag can be frustrating.'

Slowness of response by local authority social workers has been noted by other researchers (Coleman *et al.*, 1982 p.72; Wilkin *et al.*, 1984, p.36) and in the present study it was described for other groups also, e.g. the psychogeriatric service, to be discussed later. Social services departments were also criticized for their high turnover of personnel, and for their organization. As a GP put it:

> 'Social services work like a
> pyramid the wrong way up: the
> experts sitting in their offices,
> little girls out doing the work.
> Just the opposite to general
> practice!'

In defence, a social worker explains:

> '15 to 25 cases might be waiting,
> not just EMI ones. Then I have
> to select by crisis. The senior
> social worker would do as much as
> he could if no-one else were
> available.'

Another social worker with experience of management explained possible reasons for slow SSD response:

1. The poor quality of referrals; the message may lack clarity or precision.

2. Poor processing of applications, e.g. the person taking the original phone call may have little idea of how to deal with it.

3. The office procedure may be slow, e.g. if senior social workers do all the allocating at a weekly meeting.

3.1.2 Variable response of the primary health care team

One LASW felt this was the biggest difficulty facing the services. As GPs themselves pointed out:

> 'It's easy to spot when the
> dementia is gross, but we
> probably miss mild cases quite
> often.'

> 'It's hard to assess on the

> doctor's first visit, the family
> can hide it, and it gets missed.'

Other GPs emphasized their passive response:

> 'There are dementing elderly I
> don't know about. But I can't
> knock on any door. Some doctors
> won't even act at *relatives'*
> *request.'*

> 'I work on an *ad hoc* basis, *not* a
> preventive basis. Most GPs are
> somewhere between the two
> extremes. The whole morning
> surgery, for instance is on-demand
> medicine. If I'm asked by
> relatives, I say "Go back and tell
> your relative I'll call, with your
> consent." It usually works: I
> rarely have to resort to barging
> in.'

Some of the problem of the delayed response was attributed
to the slowness of the relatives or carers in coming forward.
Some informants considered this put strain on carers rather than
patients, but not all GPs agreed that the problem existed.

> 'Late referrals don't matter. If
> no-one has noticed, there can't be
> a problem.

> 'I'm sure there are some I don't
> know about. They crack when the
> relatives can't cope. The acute
> episode is not the onset of
> dementia, but the crisis is a cry
> for help. I'm not really worried.
> It's a self-appointing system: the
> relatives should say, except when
> the patient lives alone (when) the
> neighbours will alert me.'

A third GP considered that 'the delay didn't matter', then
capped it with a story when it clearly had done, the carer having
to resign from a good job.

There was considerable criticism of GPs' approaches to dementing elderly patients from other groups of workers, notably from social work staff. Several said that GPs ignore dementia: they 'put everything down to old age'. As one voluntary agency worker put it, 'As they can't cure it, they ignore the social aspects'. And a social service manager adds, 'They don't attend case conferences. I'm not sure that they read what we send them'.

Frequent criticism of the GPs' role is also reported from the study by Coleman *et al.*:

> 'GPs as a whole did not appear to
> have adequately grasped the role
> of 'key worker' and co-ordinator of
> services which other agencies
> expected of them as the usual
> first referral point for new
> patients.' (1982, p.65)

Further criticisms centred on their unwillingness to act upon the discovery of dementia, especially in referring the patient to the psychogeriatric services. There was evidence from both sides of this relationship that it was difficult to work with total efficiency: no doubt the novelty of the service contributed to this. So did training:

> 'GP training is inadequate. They
> have very little exposure to
> geriatrics, let alone
> psychogeriatrics.' (Consultant)

> 'The treatable causes of dementia
> are stressed, but one doesn't
> learn the services available.
> Students are only interested in
> diagnosis.' (GP trainee)

Other remarks suggested that patients (or their relatives) might be slow to come forward with the symptoms of dementia, for a variety of reasons: fear of the stigma of mental illness, an unwillingness to 'trouble the doctor' or a refusal to accept that benefits might follow. Some suggested that people were especially unlikely to attempt the benefits of medical intervention if dementia was known to 'run in the family'.

Things may have improved somewhat: one GP (who had been qualified seventeen years) claimed never to have seen an acute psychiatric patient while an undergraduate! Another points out the practicalities of the system in which they work:

> 'GPs either work with a system
> when they say, "I will refer
> everyone" which logjams the
> system, or they ration referrals.
> I could overburden the services
> here: but what good would that
> do?'

Other members of the primary health care team potentially have a very valuable role to play in the care of the dementing elderly, but their organizational structure usually prevents them from becoming familiar with many dementing patients. Nurse members of the team (Health Visitors, District Nursing Sisters) are organized in a variety of ways, yet few of those interviewed in the present study could identify more than a handful of dementing elderly among their patients. Nevertheless, as will be shown in the next chapter, the contribution of HVs and DNs to the management of individual cases could be immense. Both groups felt that their training suffered from a lack of psychiatric input and they themselves felt poorly equipped to deal with dementing elderly people. There was considerable feeling that all professional groups who made large numbers of home visits often missed the signs of dementia.

Several informants would have liked better co-ordination within the primary health care team, and one or two favoured the creation of a crisis intervention team.

3.1.3 Role of the CPN

One notable innovation in primary health care in very recent years has been the introduction of community psychiatric nurses. In the present study, like that of two areas by Coleman *et al.* (1982, p.64) the CPN service was better developed in one location than the other.

In the city, the creation of a geriatric team of CPNs had been carried through some time prior to the research. A team of 3 or 4 CPNs were well established in their base at the local geriatric hospital, and another CPN was on temporary attachment to the health centre where the sample's primary health care team was based. Each of the hospital-based CPNs had a caseload of 40 patients with dementia, a far higher number than were found in the caseloads of almost all the rest of the sample. In the town, a solitary CPN in post was given responsibility for elderly patients during the course of the research. No comparable figures are therefore possible, but the experience of a CPN in a neighbouring town is instructive. She serves a population of 22,000, and 36 GPs. She has only three elderly dementing patients, explaining 'with so many GPs, it is difficult to establish regular contact'.

As with the CPNs investigated by Coleman *et al.*, their work received considerable praise from other workers.

> 'An excellent service.' (Consultant)

> 'We've always worked with them
> quite well.' (LASW)

Both the psychogeriatrician and the GPs in the city noted with satisfaction the increasing use of the CPN to short-circuit referrals. Two of the GPs stated:

> 'Now we refer to our CPN, the
> consultant may take more notice of
> her. It's much more satisfactory
> to have her as a member of the
> team. Now we see her at least
> every week. We've not referred
> anyone to the consultant since she
> joined our team.'

> 'She'll assess if there's an acute
> problem, and discuss it with the
> consultant: a major problem has
> melted away.'

Other informants drew attention to the manpower limitations of the CPN service: 'Not enough of them' (HV) and 'They do their best with their limited resources' (Nurse Manager). There was also some criticism, from a GP and a social work manager, of their feedback and their contact with other agencies.

Part of the problem in the urban area may have arisen from the CPNs' scattered location: those serving groups of psychiatric patients other than the demented elderly were distributed throughout several other psychiatric units around the city. As one put it:

> 'Where we are based is a mystery
> to some GPs..... if we were
> together, our specialized

knowledge would be available to
all.'

The nurse manager for CPNs in the urban area points out additional advantages of better management liaison; in-service training, peer support within the group and secretarial assistance would also be possible if the CPNs were gathered on one site.

3.1.4 Physically fit dementing old people

A third difficulty for domicillary workers concerned the identification and treatment of physically fit demented old people. This group undoubtedly cause problems for all those engaged in domiciliary care. In the words of one informant, 'It is harder to engage the services and the individual can cause more uproar'. Several examples will be given in the next chapter.

3.1.5 Out of hours assistance

A final difficulty concerned the need on occasion to provide care out of office hours for people living at home; not all services could answer this need. Criticisms on this score were levelled at a number of agencies, especially the home care service in the town, which was provided on a fairly inflexible basis. In the city, on the other hand, a twilight and emergency weekend service was in action, and other improvements under discussion. The CPN service in the town was also criticized on this basis. In the city their service was probably functioning effectively because of the voluntary overtime hours worked by the CPNs. The voluntary sector was not considered to fill the gaps in the operation of the statutory services, in this respect.

3.2 Day Care

Day care was well represented in both locations with a total of 19 informants from a variety of agencies.

Generally there was a strong feeling that more day care was needed, and more transport, and one GP considered more day care was 'top priority'. But there was little agreement on what *kind* of additional day care was required. While day hospitals were widely praised, some informants were hostile to the very idea. A consultant from outside the area, for example, is planning to develop services considerably without creating a day hospital.

Some difficulties are historical, arising out of the

institution's novelty, and the lack of experience of staff. The role of day care agencies is not always clear. When first set up, day hospitals received patients whose needs might have been better provided for in the less theraputically-oriented, and less expensive, setting of the day centre. As the sister-in-charge of one put it,

> 'Some patients have been here a
> long time ...... over half need
> tender loving care and diversion
> rather than assessment.'

The view of the psychogeriatrician is different:

> 'It is over-loaded with people
> who should be in short-term
> residential care.'

Secondly, the staff suffer from the novelty of their situation. Psychogeriatric day hospitals are relatively new institutions whose rules have been established only recently. Staff vacancies are therefore unlikely to be filled by recruits already experienced in their working. Sisters-in-charge may feel particularly isolated, and there are difficulties in communication with primary health care teams, and with patients' relatives. The involvement of psychogeriatric day hospitals in nurse training appears to be slight.

Thirdly, difficulties are reported in co-ordinating statutory and voluntary sector contributions to day care, to best effect. In the city, the voluntary sector's efforts have expanded from a discouraging beginning ('regarded with suspicion' according to one informant) to providing a day centre on three or four days a week, plus a sitting service for relatives; but a GP pointed out the latter's limitations:

> 'The focus is on help to
> *relatives*, not patients.'

Thus those living alone, or in residential care and needing the stimulus of a day centre, might be losing out.

In the town, voluntary sector activity in providing day care was much less well developed. Indeed, an attempt to establish a lunch-club in a nearby village had foundered. There was no recognized voluntary day centre which catered for demented old people.

3.3   Hospital and residential care

Among the interviewed sample were sixteen people whose job involved the provision of hospital and residential care: four psychogeriatricians, three geriatricians, three hospital social workers and social work managers, three managers or deputy managers of local authority elderly persons' homes, two proprietors of private residential homes for the elderly, and an official of a local authority housing development.   Fourteen per cent of the whole sample (equally divided between the two locations, and between doctors and others) felt that residential care was under-provided.   Six informants felt that the shortage of residential provision was the single most significant gap in service provision.   As with day care, however, there was little consensus on what *kind* of additional resources were needed.

There were major differences in organization in both areas in both psychogeriatric services and in local authority residential provision for dementing elderly people.

3.3.1 Hospital Services

In the city, the psychogeriatrician runs a dementia-only service, which an administrator approves of:

> 'It seemed reasonable when he was
> first appointed.   There was simply
> too much to do, and he limited his
> actions accordingly.'

The psychogeriatrician himself says:

> 'There are no joint beds with
> geriatricians.   A joint unit is
> not a crying need, though it might
> be useful.   The district requires
> a comprehensive psychogeriatric
> service, with a full-time psycho-
> geriatrician.   I was appointed for
> three sessions.   With that I
> couldn't run a comprehensive or
> even an adequate dementia service.
> Given my present resources, if I
> gave 6 sessions instead of three,
> what else could I do?'

> 'No-one wants to mix EMIs and

dementias. The problems of the
dementias get in the way of the
others. There are more demented
in-patients; they would swamp the
functionally ill.'

A consultant geriatrician supports him:

'A one-door policy is attractive
in some ways, e.g. it stops people
being shunted about. But the
service as it is can be flexible,
e.g. psychogeriatric patients can
attend the geriatric day hospital
for specific purposes. But it
stops people thinking.
Responsibility for sorting people
out should lie with the primary
health care team. There are not
enough patients for a joint unit.
Negotiations can be very simple:
you can have 'negotiations at
consultant level' when the two
consultants can split the task.'

Other voices oppose such a system. A consultant from
outside the area does not favour a dementia only service, for the
following reasons:

1. The consultant has to fight for the full
   complement of beds. Dementia alone won't have the
   status.

2. The morale and training of staff benefit if some
   patients recover.

3. There's a turn-around of beds. Otherwise the
   general psychiatrists cream off all the nice old
   ladies with depression.

Another consultant suggests a compromise:

'Patients could move between two
capsules of a building, providing
two sorts of care: one more
psychiatric, one for physical and

medical problems.'

The local CHC secretary goes further:

> 'The EMI fall between the two
> schools of geriatrics psychiatry.
> We should move away from having
> separate geriatric units: we want
> "beds for the elderly sick".'

Certainly there was evidence of much dementia in the geriatricians' wards. One consultant, by his own 'rough-and-ready' calculations, had 69 dementing patients. Another considered that 'the vast bulk' of his 127 long-stay patients were dementing. A geriatric social worker reckoned up to 8 of her referrals each month were dementing.

3.3.2 Local authority services

Local authority residential services face similar problems of many dementing clients with no clear-cut model of service organization providing the best solution. The urban SSD is firmly committed to the segregation of elderly people with dementia in separate homes. The SSD serving the small town has no such provision, which leads to a substantial amount of critical comment.

> 'The major gap is that residents
> in our EPHs are fitter than in
> other authorities. They don't
> provide for people with dementia.
> Severely demented old people may
> not be fit enough for EPHs, but
> too fit for hospital.' (Social
> work team leader)

> 'We need somewhere between a Part
> III home and a psychiatric
> hospital.' (Residential social
> worker)

> 'The main problem is the people
> who cannot live alone, but are not
> suitable for Part III, because for
> example they wander too much, yet
> they are not bad enough for

hospital.' (GP)

'There are no separate EMI homes.
There are lots of demented people
in the EPHs. I get them when
they are physically ill, as the
psychogeriatric service is so
bad.' (Consultant geriatrician)

However, some demented people *are* admitted to EPHs. A new
Part III home opened while interviewing for this research was in
progress, and a quarter of the first 32 admissions were
considered to be dementing by the officer-in-charge.

'They are generally fit, and not
agitated. They don't present
major management problems.'

A local social work team leader points out that the
residents are easier to manage if they begin to dement after
arrival, as they will have had time to impose their personality
on the home. Those who are already dementing on arrival are less
easy to accept.

Only one voice - a residential social worker's - was raised
against segregated homes for the elderly.

'I don't like them. The residents
have no way to improve.'

However, the limitations of the segregated EPH which served
the city were pointed out by several. Admission is restricted to
those who are physically fit and relatively mobile; those who
need assistance in walking may not be considered for admission.
The officer-in-charge herself feels the need for a further
halfway house:

'It would have been better if this
place had been built for 24, not
36. But what's lacking is a
smaller house, midway between here
and an EPH, for the mildly
confused, kept at a better level.
It could be used as an assessment
and short-term care centre, too.'

3.3.3.   Size of units

The question of the most desirable size of units comes up during several interviews.   Invariably the preference was, as with the officer quoted above, for relatively small units.

> 'I envisage small houses of up to four to six people, as in mental handicap.' (Nurse manager)

> 'I'm committed to small homely joint-staffed units of up to 10 beds.' (Social work manager)

> 'I'd like smaller homes: the smaller it is, the easier to manage. It may seem dearer to run.' (CPN)

> 'Many demented old people could be accommodated in a sheltered environment, with sufficient nursing, training and care. Training is needed to minimize incontinence.   It's better than physically-oriented   wards.' (Consultant geriatrician)

> 'I don't want beds for continuing care in hospitals.   There is no reason why demented old people need to be on a hospital ward.   We need units of 10 to 12 beds.   Part III is wrong: the units are too large.   We needn't make the same mistakes.'

This last quotation was from a consultant psychogeriatrician in another part of the country, who is attempting to put that policy into action.

3.3.4   Short-term care

Short-term care is a particularly problematic area.   Some informants were sceptical of its benefits.

'Nice for relatives, but may be
unsettling for patients.' (GP)

'Holiday relief beds are not
really working. Patients may go
out worse than they came in.'
(Nurse manager)

A welfare assistant had had previous experience as a
residential social worker: 'Some of our residents went into
short-term care and never came back'.

Nevertheless, there was considerable enthusiasm for more
short-term care: twelve informants (from a wide variety of
agencies) were in favour. One GP felt that if more short-term
care were available, families would be encouraged to provide more
caring themselves.

The form such additional short-term caring should take was
more controversial. A hospital social worker, while not urging
an increase in provision, felt it should be in a more pleasant
location than in hospital. A voluntary sector worker said:

'Carers need a night service,
where they can book their relative
in for the odd night. A separate
night centre is not appropriate:
it may be disorienting for
clients. It's better to have a
good bookable form of respite
care, e.g. in an established
residential home.'

As mentioned earlier, the officer-in-charge of the Part III
home specializing in dementia in the city favoured a home for
less demented residents, which could double as an assessment and
short-term care centre. She originally had two short-term beds
at her residential home, but lack of demand had reduced this to
one.

'The short-term residents I have
had here have been more able, and
thus more disturbed by being kept
with the long-stay, more demented
residents.'

A GP favours a separate hostel (not a hospital) for short-
term care. Ideally this would not cater for assessment or long-

term residents, whose needs are somewhat different.

In the small town, GP beds are available in the community hospital and this arrangement was widely praised. Such a service is clearly local, and the only doubts concerned the appropriate skills of some of the nursing staff.

3.3.5 Private homes

Residential care is provided by a number of private residential homes in the study area. Informants suggested that many provide a poor quality of care: standards are widely held to be more variable than in the state sector. In particular, concern was expressed over the following points:

1. assessment might not always be made at the time of entry into care;

2. there are problems of surveillance, especially in view of the rapid rise in numbers of private residential homes;

3. there is little incentive to provide accommodation of good standard;

4. referral to other agencies (e.g. CPNs) was not always carried out appropriately. People may deteriorate needlessly in such circumstances.

3.3.6 A variety of options

Reviewing the spectrum of residential care, the need is above all for a variety of options, with sufficient capacity to permit demented elderly people to move among them as necessary, while keeping the element of disruption of their lives to a minimum. In the existing system, much movement is perceived as blocked, with each institution protected by its waiting list.

Some relevant remarks are worth noting here:

'Residential care is often
deferred for those with relatives.
The residential services
discriminate against them.' (SSD
researcher)

'It's difficult to judge if direct

> admissions to the specialist Part
> III homes are successful. I'd
> rather admit to an ordinary Part
> III first.' (Social worker)

> 'If admission to Part III cannot
> be achieved, I have to sell the
> patient to the geriatricians.'
> (GP)

Movement between institutions is thus difficult.

> 'We cannot always get our
> residents admitted to
> psychogeriatric beds.'
> (Residential social worker)

> 'It can be difficult to get EPHs
> to take patients back, e.g. after
> surgery.' (Geriatrician)

> 'Because of the demand for
> psychiatric beds, hospital
> transfers are not possible, except
> at times for the geriatricians.'
> (Psychogeriatrician)

The result is that 'healthy' movement within the system may be blocked, with transfers only possible by barter arrangement. This will be discussed further in the next chapter.

3.4   Informal support

Numerous informants from a variety of agencies considered that relatives concealed dementia on account of the fear of the stigma of mental illness.

> 'They fear the hereditary taint,
> being classed as mad. One
> relative came from abroad to say
> there was no other madness in her
> family than her sister. She'd
> been rehearsing it in English for
> weeks.' (Voluntary sector worker)

> 'Some people are frightened of

>dementia. Families hide it for a
long time.' (Social worker)

>'At first, the elderly person is
just seen as naughty. Until it
becomes a crisis, they don't see
it as a referral to me.' (Social
worker)

>'It's OK if the neighbours can't
see it.' (Consultant)

But other reasons add to the reticence with which dementia is concealed, and formal services mobilized. One is fear of 'troubling the doctor'.

>'You don't like to trouble the
doctor, you hope the problem will
go away.' (Community nurse)

>'Relatives may acquiesce in the
GP's inactivity.' (Nurse manager)

Another reason is that action is perceived as pointless: relatives may not be aware of what help is available. Sometimes the family may not act until a crisis occurs, such as incontinence or heightened awareness following a visit from distant relatives. Signs of growing dementia may be ignored if it was reckoned to 'run in the family'.

Often the contribution of neighbours is crucial: Wilkin *et al* (1984) found that friends and neighbours were the carers in 9% of cases. Several GPs confirmed this impression:

>'Neighbours are the best form of
voluntary help. Some maintain
demented old people in the
community.'

>'Without the help of neighbours in
many cases, the services couldn't
cope.'

>'The most valuable resource of
all.'

Comments contrasting informal helping systems in the city

and the countryside were necessarily impressionistic, but differences were by no means clear-cut.

A GP and a nursing assistant in the small town felt that the smaller the community, the more likely neighbours were to help. A community nurse in the city stated:

> 'There's a good neighbour gap in the city. Lots of unobtrusive help is available in the villages, people are more prepared to 'nanny' the elderly. Here neighbours keep more to themselves. This is not always a disadvantage: children are *expected* to take responsibility in rural areas, but this may be difficult. Outsiders can sometimes cope *better* than relatives.'

A GP felt that referral was more likely in a small town.

> 'Most of the problems get drawn to our attention. People in the city are more likely to fall through the net.'

But other informants felt that small-town life involved a closing of the ranks, which might actually inhibit the speedy and efficient deployment of services.

> 'In the villages, the neighbours cover dementia up.' (Nursing assistant)

> 'Relatives ask later in rural areas.' (CPN)

3.5 Education

Just over a quarter of the informants made comments on the appropriateness or otherwise of their training for their role in treating dementing old people. Generally those who had their training in the last five years or so felt it had been appropriate; those who had trained longer ago felt it had not.

Comments on GPs' training were given earlier, in the section on domiciliary care. Consultants were reckoned to need more training in management, and the status of the relevant medical specialisms needed to be raised.

Other groups (OTs, physios, home care assistants and staff in private residential homes) were all reckoned to need more relevant training. But most of the comment concerned the training of nurses. This ranged over several aspects, from the difficulty of working in a psychogeriatric day hospital ('Not seen as a proper job') to the difficulty of providing minimal training for nursing auxilliaries.

3.6   Differences between the two areas

Overall the patterning of problems in service provision differed considerably between the two areas, although there was some overlap.

In the urban area the principal perceived need was for additional residential care places, especially in hospitals.

The restricted availability of the psychogeriatrician has already been spelt out. When he had been appointed, eight years previously, patients in his long-stay beds were 'a hotchpotch' who had been there up to 25 years.

> 'I halved the number of beds and
> made the two wards one long-stay
> and one short-stay. There was a
> complete turnover in the first
> year, but now they are silted up.'

> 'Many patients would benefit from
> adequate assessment. Some are
> difficult to distinguish, e.g.
> between organic brain syndrome and
> behaviour problems. But almost
> none of these have been admitted
> in the last two years: admissions
> now are for emergency relief
> only.'

Both the consultant and the hospital social worker would prefer assessment to take place in a more pleasant environment than at present obtains, a ward in the geriatric hospital that started life as a workhouse. A nurse manager makes the obvious point that a lack of adequate assessment facilities has a knock-on effect of producing more work for day care, CPNs, GPs and the social services. The consultant psychogeriatrician adds that it is also seldom possible to take over patients in the beds of other consultants. This is a particularly severe problem with respect to the geriatricians.

Other informants pointed out the lack of sufficient places in local authority residential homes and day hospitals. There were particularly difficulties in both areas when patients from outlying villages needed residential care which could not be provided close enough for their relatives to visit easily.

A major problem reported by six people in the small town sample (but no-one in the city) concerned the difficulty of recruiting OTs and physiotherapists. Another problem which appeared relatively greater in the town was the quality of the home care service: both availability limited largely to office hours, and the financial charges which deterred some of the most needy from using the service. Levels of training and morale also appeared lower than in the city.

The need to provide a local service for outlying villages was even more of an issue than in the city. The development of the voluntary sector appeared in general more hesitant than in the city.

3.7. Summary

This sample of 85 service managers and workers, drawn mainly from two contrasting areas within the same health authority, produce a wide range of critical comments concerning local services for dementing elderly people.

Problems identified in the domiciliary services centre around a number of issues: the slowness of response to referrals, especially among local authority social service departments; the variable response of primary health care teams, where the passivity of the GPs' stance was considered at times to delay effective service deployment; providing effective help for fit dementing elderly people; and the restriction of some domiciliary services to office hours. CPNs were acknowledged to provide an extremely effective service, and the difference in its level of development in the two areas under study noted.

A need for more day care was strongly voiced, but there was considerable disagreement in the kind of additional day care resources needed.

The hiving-off by the psychogeriatrician in the city area of a dementia-only service followed his perception of the impossibility of providing a full psychogeriatric service given the resources available to him. Opinions were mixed concerning the wisdom of his decision: much dementia was considered to exist among patients in health service units elsewhere.

Local authority residential services for elderly people are

faced with difficult choices, concerning the size of units provided, and the degree of integration to be sought between demented and non-demented residents. In the city one Part III home provided exclusively for demented residents; in the town demented residents were spread around existing homes. Neither system was reckoned to work particularly well.

Short-term care, and the appropriate provision for residents with dementia in private residential homes, were other areas of concern. What appears desirable is a range of residential options, among which elderly people with dementia can move freely, with minimal dislocation to their lives.

The role of informal sources of help is not always seen as benign: relatives may inhibit the deployment of service help. Neighbours were sometimes a vital contribution to the network of help.

Finally, some professionals felt that their training, if undertaken many years previously, failed to equip them adequately to deal with dementia; and various differences emerged between perceived shortcomings in the two locations.

6 STUDYING DEMENTIA CAREERS

6.1 The sample

How realistic were the comments and criticisms made in the last chapter by those involved in providing, managing and planning services for dementing elderly people? To test the reality of their comments, a sample of dementing elderly people were identified and their 'dementia careers' traced and reconstructed. Relatives and other informal carers were not approached due to the practical constraints of time and resources, and because the views of relatives have been sought by several other enquiries (e.g. Levin *et al.*, 1983; Gilleard, 1984, Gilhooly, 1984; George and Gwyther, 1986).

Six agencies (the psychogeriatric service, the social service department and one general practice, in the city and in the town) were asked to note new cases of dementia aged 65 or more referred to them during a period of three months in the summer of 1985. Other names were drawn from the current caseload.

A sample of 20 cases (10 new referrals, 10 on-going cases) from each agency was planned, but this did not prove possible to achieve. The general practices and the SSDs received few new dementia cases during the period of the field-work, so the bulk of their sample was drawn from existing cases. Even so, both SSDs fell well short of the desired total, as did cases identified by the psychogeriatric service in the town. As the town itself did not provide enough cases, another small town nearby was included in the study area, along with the surrounding villages. Table 6.1 gives details of the final sample size.

Table 6.1 Sample sources

	General Practice		Psychogeriatric Service		Social Services Department	
	New referrals	On-going cases	New referrals	On-going cases	New referrals	On-going cases
City	3	18	15	7	3	10
Town	4	15	5	9	5	6

Initial interviews were held with a worker in the identifying agency. During the following four months, other agencies providing care for the subjects were identified and interviews held with the most involved member(s) of staff. An average of 3.43 informants were interviewed for each of the subjects. Four months after the initial interview, a final interview was held with the initial informant, or in a few cases with a worker who had become more centrally involved with the elderly subject during the previous four months. Altogether, as comprehensive a picture of the subject's dementia career was constructed, stretching back retrospectively in as much detail as possible, as well as covering the four months of active field-work.

Altogether the survey drew on 89 informants, 55 in the city and 35 in the town. (One person worked in both locations.) Many were individuals who had also been surveyed in the investigation of the adequacy of local services described in the previous chapter. Table 6.2 lists their agencies.

Table 6.2 Informants' agencies

	City	Town
Psychogeriatric Service	12	10
Social Service Department	18	13
General Practice	11	6
Geriatric Service	9	2
Voluntary Sector	4	2
Other	1	2
	55	35

The diagnosis of dementia was the subject of some discussion in a few cases, some of which were discarded in the course of the field-work. Of the 100 finally accepted for the sample, precise diagnosis remained unclear in a number of cases throughout the duration of the field-work. The final diagnosis (performed by the author at the end of the field-work on the basis of all available evidence) is shown in Table 6.3. 85 were confirmed as dementia sufferers, including 17 for whom another psychiatric diagnosis was added. 7 were diagnosed acute confusional states, 6 given other psychiatric diagnoses, and no diagnosis could be made for two. The difficulties of precise diagnosis which were encountered underline the problem of the epidemiologist's task outlined in Chapter Two.

Table 6.3 Diagnosis by identifying agency

	Total	GP	Psycho-geriatric	SSD
Dementia	68	29	24	15
Dementia & other psychiatric conditions	17	7	8	2
Acute confusional state	7	3	2	2
Pseudo-dementia	2	0	1	1
Other psychotic condition	1	0	0	1
Neurotic condition	3	0	1	2
No precise diagnosis	2	1	0	1

It illustrates too the complexity of the task facing the services in deciding just what are the problems presented to them.

25 of the sample were men, 75 women. 17 were aged 65-74, 58 75-84, and 25 over the age of 85. 13 of this oldest group were among those identified by GPs.

6 were single, 45 married, and 49 widowed or divorced. A majority of new cases, but a minority of on-going cases were widowed or divorced. Nearly two-thirds of the men, but only a minority of the women, were married. Among the widowed and divorced, women outnumbered men by over five to one.

An attempt was made to assign each subject to middle or working class on the basis of subject's occupation, spouse's occupation, or life-style. This proved possible in only 63 cases (33 middle, 30 working). The working class group appears over-represented in the sub-sample identified by the psychogeriatric service, as shown on Table 6.4.

At the time of the first interview, 41 of the sample were living with their spouse, 28 alone and 15 with a child (or son-in-law or daughter-in-law). 14 were in institutions and 2 with non-relatives. Fifteen of the men were living with their wives and only four alone. In contrast 26 of the women were living with their husbands, and 24 alone. All but one of those living in institutions were women.

Table 6.4 Social class

	Middle class	Working class	Not possible to assign class
City	20	18	18
Town	13	12	19
Men	5	9	11
Women	28	21	26
Identifying agency:			
Psychogeriatrics	11	16	9
GP	13	8	19
SSD	9	6	9

The preponderance of women in the households of dementing elderly people is marked. 26 women subjects live with their husbands. 15 men subjects live with their wives; other female relatives are present in three of these households. Two men and seven women subjects live with their daughter (plus son-in-law in four cases). Two men and four women live with their daughter-in-law (plus son in five cases). None lives with an unaccompanied son or son-in-law. The preponderance of female carers resembles the situation described elsewhere.

Living conditions varied from the ideal to the crux of the problem.

> Case 084. A woman of 76, had been living with her husband a hundred miles from the study area. Their son and daughter-in-law lived in the

next county. When the son and daughter-in-law moved to the rural study area, they sought and obtained a house which could be converted to include a 'granny annex'. They had had considerable support from their local SSD, who made the referral to the study area SSD. When the family moved in, the involvement of the home care service was initially delayed as they were coping so well.

Case 099. A woman of 80, long widowed, living as the tenant of a flat in a private house. She had been dementing almost two years, becoming an increasing nuisance to the landlady and physically threatening to the landlady's mother (who was older than she was). Despite the attempts of several services, no-one has been able to persuade or compel her to move.

6.2. Initial recognition of dementia

Some of the difficulties concerning the recognition and precise measurement of dementia have been set out in Chapter 2. One of the problems is that of timing the initial onset. Estimates of relatives and doctors have been shown to be widely divergent (Gilleard, 1984). In the present study, the evidence from GPs confirms this impression. They are themselves in a poor position to provide accurate estimates. Much of their own knowledge of patients is gleaned from relatives. Even when they form an impression that dementia may be present, they do not always record the fact. Some people were known to be dementing without it being recorded in the GP's case-notes. Referral to specialist agencies may be delayed still further.

Case 004. A woman of 78 living with her husband of about the same age. First recording of dementia in the case-notes in April 1985. At interview (three months later) the GP could recall earlier unrecorded conversations when her symptoms had been discussed. But her husband did not want a psychiatrist involved, and the GP saw other medical services being provided only through that channel.

It may not be too much of an over-simplification to suggest that often the diagnosis of dementia in the GP's mind may actually correspond to referral to the psychogeriatrician. Even then the separation from dementia from other psychiatric conditions may be difficult. Indeed, this may be seen as the purpose of the referral.

Estimates of the period dementing are possible for 26 of the GP-identified cases living in the community. Only one had been dementing less than a year, and 15 had been dementing for at least three years. These included two who were estimated to have been dementing for ten years; the affairs of one of them had been under the Court of Protection for that time. Two had been dementing for long periods in Part III homes: one for six years and the other for just over three years. (The latter had never seen a psychiatrist.) Five lived alone.

The onset of dementia was usually estimated by the GP himself or by his predecessor, or by a close relative of the subject. In a few cases, the subject herself was the first to draw attention to the problem. Sometimes a specific event (often a physical illness) was noted as the trigger. One husband considered his wife's dementia started years previously, but that its origins went back 'as far as the London blitz'.

GPs may regard confusion in the elderly as seldom worth more than a passing mention. They notice it frequently but act upon it only rarely. As one said, 'We don't write it down. We accept that patients are confused'. In Chapter Three several studies were quoted which illustrate GPs' ignorance of their patients' symptoms.

This suggests that GPs are either incapable of, or uninterested in, identifying patients who will subsequently deteriorate mentally, with progressive dementia. Such reticence has probably a basis in practice: Bergmann *et al.* (1979) show that clinicians are poor identifiers of sufferers from progressive dementia. Dementia is often difficult to distinguish from depression. Several of the sample were anxious or depressed at the initial appearance of symptoms of dementia.

> Case 035. The original letter from the GP to the psychogeriatrician said she had been prescribed (but may not have taken) antidepressants by her previous GP. When the psychogeriatrician saw her, it was difficult for him to establish what her problems were, as she wept throughout the interview. He thought she was depressed because her memory was going.

6.3 Maintaining the demented person at home

The work of Coleman *et al.* (1982) reveals criticisms of the way GPs perform their role from other service providers for dementing old people, concerning lack of attention to the patient's problems, insufficient contact and above all adequate communication with other workers.   There was also considerable praise (p.65).

GPs are not in a particularly strong position to provide effective care themselves for their dementing patients.   Chemical treatments which have been introduced in the past few years in the hope they would delay the development of symptoms have generally fallen out of favour.   In the 40 cases in the sample identified by GPs, 16 had been prescribed medication as part of their recent treatment, although this was generally in response to conditions other than dementia.   Other interventions were far from routinely provided: only seven patients or their carers had received psychotherapy or reassurance and six had been physically examined.

In a number of cases, the GP appeared to have done nothing, or simply to have referred the patient to a colleague in the primary health care team, or to another agency.   Table 6.5 gives the details.   Not all agencies were accepted by the patient (or carer).   The sparse use of agencies other than the psychogeriatrician among the town sample is notable.

**Table 6.5 Agencies to which GPs referred patients
at the most recent consultation (GP identified patients only)**

	City	Town	Total
Psychogeriatrician	3	11	14
District Nursing Sister	3	3	6
C.P.N.	4	1	5
Bath nurse	4	Not available	4
Geriatrician	3	1	4
Social Service Department	3	1	4
Voluntary organization day centre	3	Not available	3
Continence adviser	1	1	2
Physiotherapist	1	0	1
Meals-on-wheels	1	0	1

The survey of professional workers described in Chapter Five showed considerable agreement that GPs adopted a passive stance towards patients' help-seeking behaviour, and that their response to dementia symptoms were far from uniform. Field-work observation confirmed both these claims.

GPs adopt a passive stance in three ways:

1. They leave the initiative in seeking consultations to patients, occasionally to patients' relatives. There appeared little evidence of screening visits, although one newly-appointed GP was 'popping in' to all his elderly patients.

2. GPs do not always advise or act upon suspected dementia, and may ignore it altogether. One carer saw three GPs within 3 weeks; they appeared hypnotized by the need to regulate the patient's potentially dangerous drug regime, and none raised the question of help with dementia, although the patient had just moved into the area. In another case the GP justified his attitude of not raising the subject of dementia partly because the patient's wife had an aggressive personality which inhibited the GP's actions.

3. GPs may prefer, at least initially, to look for a physical cause if the symptoms of dementia are noticed.

It may be that dementia is sometimes a 'negotiated diagnosis' as has been described for mental handicap (Booth, 1978). Patients or carers can however sometimes influence a GP's actions. One said of his 80-year-old patient, 'I wouldn't have referred her to the CPN if her husband had not asked, as she was clean, fed, well clothed and cared for. If physical problems had arisen, I'd have involved the DNS. But I would not have asked on my own initiative, as they appeared to be coping reasonably well'.

Several cases illustrate the widespread variation in GPs' response to dementia.

> Case 001. The social worker says, 'I might have adopted another approach with a different GP. This one takes a 'non-interventionist' stance, which prevents me involving the HV or DNS'.

Sometimes other workers are able to use such variations for their own purposes.

> Case 040. Is a resident in a Part III home. The Officer-in-Charge says, 'When she became aggressive, I phoned the psychogeriatrician's

social worker. We decided to ask the
consultant to ask the GP to review her
medication'. (Why not ask the GP directly?)
'He's new. He doesn't know her. And I don't
want her made into a zombie by medication.'
Earlier another worker involved in the care
of this patient had got her referred to the
psychogeriatrician by taking her along on a
day chosen deliberately when a locum GP was
in the surgery, as the regular GP had refused
to refer her previously.

Sometimes it is a relative who resists referral. Husbands of
two subjects (reckoned to be stubborn, difficult men) resisted
medical (and especially psychiatric) referral. Another refused
to go into hospital, so his wife had to go instead.

Case 097. A woman who demented following an
unsuccessful cataract operation. Her husband
refused a warden assisted home. Later he had
a stroke but refused to go into hospital.
His wife deteriorated further, and despite
attempts at providing maximum home care, she
was admitted to psychiatric hospital a few
days later.

After the GP, the primary health care team member most
involved with dementing elderly patients is the District Nursing
Sister. Norman (1982, pp.25-6) describes the variety of their
organizational style.

DNS's were heavily involved in at least half-a-dozen of the
sample. Coleman *et al.* (1982, p.45) found that activities and
philosophies of DNS's could sometimes overlap with other team
members, and this happened in some cases in the present sample.

Case 012. A widow of 86 was discharged from hospital
after a fall. She was very deaf and
difficult to deal with. She was incontinent,
with oedematous legs. The CPN found it
difficult to collaborate with the DNS over
her nursing care, and unwilling to provide it
all, as she felt it was primarily a physical
nursing job, and the patient was becoming too
dependent on her.

Case 007. A woman of 79. Both she and her husband had
psychiatric histories. She has been known to
both medical and social services over a

number of years. She has attended geriatric day hospital for five years and has been making increasing use of Part III. Her husband has fought a long campaign to be rehoused away from their suburban council flat, to be nearer the city centre. Concern grew because of her poor attendance at day hospital and apparent physical deterioration. The social workers (both in hospital and local authority) wrote to the Community Physician to press her claim for a warden-assisted flat near the Part III home that she used. The DNS, putting more emphasis on her physical care, wanted her admitted permanently to Part III. The MSW said 'We were willing to tolerate a greater degree of risk, emphasizing that they valued their privacy and their relationship'.

In contrast, there were several successes in the sample, where a suitable mix of services kept dementing individuals maintained at home over long periods of time.

Case 038. A local 'character' who has become a recluse. Lives in total squalor in a fairly isolated house in a village. Very fit. Looked after by a mix of statutory and voluntary services orchestrated by the next-door neighbour. Her GP (who lives nearby) reckons she has been dementing for 10 years, since her affairs came under the Court of Protection. He does not see her for several months at a time, but the home help visits twice a week and the DNS frequently. Neighbours do her shopping, and keep the place as tidy as possible.

Case 009. A single man of 79, reckoned to be dementing by his GP over a period of 10 years, living in a sheltered housing scheme with support from home help, neighbour and Part III Day Centre. Although probably of borderline intelligence, he had had a local job and was popular and well thought of. He began to deteriorate mentally and physically early in 1985 and after some resistance was admitted to the Part III home in the course of the enquiry, dying in hospital six weeks later.

Case 024. A single lady of 89 living in rural squalor with her dog. Discharged herself from hospital after falling in a fire (probably while drunk). Attended day hospital for one day only. Maintained at home with considerable support over several years with home help and neighbour's assistance. Resisting numerous invitations to try residential care, and becoming less of a problem as she finds it more difficult to get hold of alcohol.

Given certain prerequisites - good physical health, sympathetic responses from neighbours, especially the closest, and well-orchestrated domiciliary services, - even very demented and difficult people can remain at home for long periods of time. The absence of caring relatives may as in Case 038 above, actually help the old person's chances of staying at home, by increasing the likelihood of services being provided, and also reduce the opportunity for conflict within the family.

6.4   The role of the Social Services Department in domiciliary care

The two SSDs involved in this study have similarities and differences with respect to domiciliary care. Both have field work staff organized into social care and home care teams. The former are staffed by social workers and social work assistants and the latter by home care organizers and home care assistants (home helps). Both allocate referrals (other than emergency referrals) to one team or the other in a routinized manner. Differences include the staffing of social care teams, including a greater use of social work assistants with dementing elderly clients, in the town, where there are also financial barriers for potential clients of the home care service; this is in the opinion of the local SSD staff a frequent reason for refusal of the service among people who could benefit from it, as described in the previous chapter.

Existing work has shown widespread criticism of SSD involvement with dementing elderly clients. Social workers show little interest in the elderly as a client group (Norman, 1982, p. 23). Social service provision is of variable quality (Coleman, *et al.*, 1982 p.72; Wilkin *et al.*, 1984, p.36). There was considerable criticism of SSD's slowness of response in the present study, as described in the previous chapter.

The SSD teams identified 24 of the present sample. In the urban area, four were dealt with by home care teams and received largely routine care in matters such as cleaning and shopping. Nine were dealt with by the social care team and received more varied help. In four cases the social worker's initial task was a discussion of options facing the client, her relatives, and others. Indeed a great deal of the involvement of field social workers concerned directing clients towards other sources of help, rather than building and manipulating a case-work relationship. This usually occurs when a social worker's contact is enduring and long-term in its aims.

Attempts to rehouse form a specific focus in three cases. One, mentioned earlier briefly, is particularly instructive.

> Case 099. A widow of 80, living alone as a tenant of a flat in a house owned by a widow of 89 and her daughter. Referred to SSD by CPN about rehousing. She had become a nuisance to her landlady and her daughter, constantly entering their part of the house. The daughter considered she had been deteriorating for four years, and was becoming a fire risk. Despite nearly two years of social work involvement (at least six social workers had worked on the case at different times) no progress in rehousing had been made. The psychogeriatrician had been called in but felt unable to involve the Mental Health Act.

The social workers attempted to provide day care for three other clients, unsuccessfully in two of the cases. Other social work tasks involved looking after the interests of relatives; arranging short-term care for a husband in one case and checking that the school performance of grandchildren had not suffered in another.

Home care dominated the provision of the SSD in the town. Seven of the eleven clients received it, and an eighth was about to start. There was considerable resistance from clients. Two had refused home care and another had discontinued the service. Case 083 illustrates some of the difficulties in getting it accepted.

Turned down home care on the grounds of cost in October 1982. Accepted it in January 1985 after a period of short-term residential care, but went instead to her daughter's house, and SSD closed the case. She made another application in April 1985, but went into hospital almost at once.

Another case (035) shows how a flexible approach by the home care service can keep a very dependent old person at home.

A widow of 75 who lived with her daughter, attending a day hospital. After a petty quarrel a neighbour stopped helping and the psychiatric hospital social worker (who had been considering a compulsory admission) decided instead to ask the home care service to prepare her for day care. The home care organizer had to find a home help who would bend the rules and go in each day at 8.30, half an hour earlier than the normal starting time. This arrangement worked well and she was able to spend most of the last six months of her life living at home.

Two cases were the subject of considerable inter-service conflict.

Case 044. A widow of 86 who was admitted to psychiatric hospital under the Mental Health Act. She improved, and within two weeks an attempt was made to discharge her. An SSD social worker took her home for the day, although day hospital staff and the CPN felt she was not up to it, and ought to be kept in hospital. In the event, the attempt was abortive as water and electricity had not been reconnected at her home. This episode precipitated a crisis meeting between community and ward staff to establish lines of communication.

Case 093. Following a request from the consultant psychogeriatrician for social work assessment for a possible guardianship order on this widow of 65, neither the SSD nor the hospital social work department felt it was their responsibility. The matter was not resolved for three months.

A frequent source of criticism of the internal organization of SSDs is that many elderly clients are dealt with by social work assistants. This may mean not only a less skilled level of assistance is available, but also possibly a higher turnover of workers.

The two SSDs in the study are organized differently in this respect. In the city SSD, one social worker deals with nearly all 'EMI' cases herself. In the town, a social work assistant deals with most dementing cases. Is one system markedly better than another?

The impression given by these cases is that interest, enthusiasm, effort and above all *time* are essential pre-requisites for a successful social work service for this client group. SWAs can do a great deal to provide appropriate social work support for dementing elderly and their carers, as long as they bring the qualities mentioned above to their task, and can call on more skilled help as and when required.

Dementing elderly people and their carers seldom need enduring case-work skills. They need time to give vent to their feelings, some relief from the day-to-day burden of caring, and practical knowledge of what assistance is available within and outside the SSD. To that extent SWAs who are caring and committed can provide a good service.

Local difference in the deployment of services may account for some differences in tasks facing SSDs. In the urban area the CPN service is well-developed and may handle a larger proportion of dementing clients. The residue may consist of relatively intractable problems for which dementia is a dubious diagnosis.

The division of SSDs into social care and home care teams must be mentioned. It may be that once a case is allocated to one or the other, movement across is inhibited, should the initial decision have been inappropriate, or if the client's needs change. This may be particularly serious for the clients of the home care service, if dementia has not been identified at the initial referral, or if it develops subsequent to referral. Home helps are not trained to recognize its symptoms, and their clients may thus be excluded from social work assistance when this becomes necessary.

6.5 The work of the psychogeriatric service

As well as the sub-sample identified by the psychogeriatric service, a majority of other cases had been referred to the psychogeriatric service. The referring agency was identified in 67 cases: 55 by GPs, 6 by geriatricians, 3 by residential homes, and one each by an adult psychiatrist, a district nurse and a voluntary organization.

Good physical health appeared in several cases to reduce the likelihood of referral to the psychogeriatric service. Case 096 is an example.

> A widow of 88 living in sheltered housing. She complained of 'hearing voices' and was seen over the next twelve months by three GPs and various social service staff. Meals-on-wheels and day care were eventually provided, and both relatives and neighbours were helpful. Despite her growing dementia, there was no referral to the psychogeriatrician.

Sometimes adequate physical care appeared sufficient until the need waned.

> Case 026. A widow of 91. In August 1985 the Oic (Officer in charge of a local authority 'Part III' home) was considering referral as she had become too difficult to manage. But by December she had become frailer and less active, and the need had passed.

Another simply kept a low profile.

> Case 018. A widow of 84 who was living at home with her son and daughter-in-law. She was one of the original referrals to a voluntary agency and at the time of the initial field-work interview had been attending for over two years, although her GP was unaware of the fact. Later she spent two brief spells in a Part III home where subsequently the staff had difficulty recalling her.

There was considerable evidence that an open referral system would have been beneficial. In several cases, social workers wanted a psychogeriatric referral but were unable to get the GP to set it in motion. In one of these the social worker saw the GP as the only gate-keeper. In another the patient's son shared the social worker's attempts to get the GP to refer, but the GP took the view, 'I've cured her before and I'll cure her again'. In another case the Oic of a Part III home wanted a psychiatric referral but the GP blocked it. In several other cases the patient's spouse resisted psychiatric referral.

In four cases other medical specialisms were involved well before referral to the psychogeriatrician. Case 087 was one example.

> A married woman of 76 was first suspected of dementia by her previous GP in 1982. When she moved into the study area in 1983, her new GP referred her to a neurologist; during 1984 she continued to suffer from epilepsy, incontinence, and various physical symptoms. She was referred to the continence adviser and to the consultant geriatrician before the psychogeriatric service was eventually involved in mid-1985.

It is widely held that the decision as to whether to call first on the geriatrician or psychogeriatrician may be an arbitrary one, or determined by the availability of practical resources, rather than clinical features. Progression in this study from geriatrician to psychogeriatrician was generally justified on the basis of the need to exclude possible physical (and directly treatable) conditions. This certainly fits in with the (sometimes unstated) wish of relatives to exclude a psychiatric stigma if at all possible. It may be the case that such patients would be helped by earlier psychiatric involvement, and care must be taken that such involvement is not widely delayed by the search for physical causes.

In the town, the local community hospital included beds controlled by GPs. In one instance this provided a leisurely resolution of a problem over responsibility.

> Case 066. A widow of 80 was admitted to a GP bed following a stroke. She recovered slowly and the hospital staff found it difficult to cope with her confusion. Her GP rang consultant 'A'. He was unable to visit promptly and the patient was eventually examined a fortnight later by consultant 'B' who found no clear evidence of dementia and did nothing. Nine

> days later Dr 'A' again visited and found her
> disoriented and tending to confabulate. But
> she was reluctant to enter a psychiatric
> hospital, and the consultant asked his social
> worker to try. She was successful in
> persuading the patient to transfer twelve
> days later.

In the urban area, direct referral to the CPN service has
been an increasing feature of the service, and the CPN made the
initial visit in several cases. The consultant described one
example: 'The diagnosis at referral seemed adequate, and it was a
service that was needed'.

Like social workers, CPNs do much that is routine and
unspectacular in the care of dementing elderly patients:
arranging day care, and short-term care in hospital, giving
injections and monitoring physical treatment, providing support
for carers, and helping the patient and her carers to evaluate
options at each stage of the condition. In some cases they work
closely with social work colleagues in exploring and arranging
residential care in EPH's when this becomes necessary.

There are opportunities too for the use of psychotheraputic
approaches. In two cases one CPN handled family conflict at
crisis point with a deftness of touch that belied her absence of
any formal training in techniques of family conflict.

> Case 059. A widower of 80 who was cared for largely by
> one daughter. His other five children were
> described by the GP as 'a bunch of wasters
> known to the police'. On a home visit the
> CPN found several of them at their father's
> home. 'All except the one daughter were
> hostile to me. They were all at loggerheads
> with one another. There was a lot of guilt
> flying about. I felt caught up in the middle
> of a long running saga. I seemed to be
> expected to manoeuvre everyone. I was the
> only real support for the daughter.' She
> continued to support the daughter as the
> patient's carer until he was admitted to
> hospital.

> Case 076. A married woman of 78. Her husband had been
> caring for her, and almost broke under the
> strain. One day he sent her to the day
> hospital with a packed suitcase and the

> message 'Admit her'. Fortunately a bed was available, and this was done. Around this time the CPN took over the case from her predecessor, and convened a family conference at the husband's home. This established that (1) none of the relatives could provide assistance if she came home, and (2) her husband *should* have her home, but the decision must be left to him. The CPN felt he had really made up his mind that he couldn't.

Considerable evidence in this present study (noted in Chapter Three) and the study by Coleman *et al.* (1982, p.64) shows how very valuable a well-developed CPN service can be. Coleman felt it made 'a crucial difference' between the two areas he studied.

6.6 Day care

60 of the sample had experience of day care. 53 had attended one of the psychogeriatric day hospitals used (one in the urban, three in the rural area); 13 had day care at one of the six Part III homes (three in each area); one had attended a geriatric day centre, and fourteen a variety of day care schemes in the voluntary sector. Nine of these had been at a particularly appropriate and successful day centre in the city.

No examples of attendance at multi-purpose centres or travelling day hospitals were found.

Eight other people in the sample had refused day care, and altogether the attendance of 15 was brief and/or disastrous. Some of these subsequently tried again, with greater success.

> Case 028. Became aggressive at psychogeriatric day hospital on his first attendance, after his wife left, and was admitted that afternoon to a psychiatric hospital under the Mental Health Act. Two months later tried again, successfully, and subsequently attended for most of the next nine months.

Informants were asked the reasons why client contact with day care agencies had been so brief in such cases. Reasons included personality too volatile, neurotic or restless (6 cases); paranoid symptoms couldn't be handled (3 cases); mentally too competent or well enough cared for (3 cases); too weak or lethargic (3 cases); behaviour too anti-social (2 cases); patient hostile to hospitals (2 cases); too middle class (2 cases); carer unwilling to relinquish role (2 cases).

Several others wanted to attend but were unable to because of a waiting list or because of difficulties of access.

In the city clients have a choice of two types of day care: a psychogeriatric day hospital and a day centre run by a voluntary agency. Workers can distinguish between clients and refer to the appropriate place, the more dependant to the day hospital:

> Case 032. A man of 82. The CPN says, 'I arranged for him to come to the day hospital. This is because firstly there are not many places at the day centre, and secondly because he's angry and grumpy at home. It's more appropriate for him to come to the day hospital as he's a management problem at home'. The voluntary day centre was assumed to be less able to handle his behaviour.

> Case 004. A woman of 78. Her CPN says, 'At my first home visit, I decided to contact the day centre, as (1) it was less trouble to use a car rather than an ambulance, and (2) they have a better staff ratio, and the patients have less severe problems, and (3) she wouldn't fit in at the day hospital. She'd be more distressed and might become too muddled. Her mental capacity is too high'.

These comments indicate the value of the choice of day care regimes, especially between the potentially intense regime of the day hospital, with its focus on assessment and rehabilitation, and the more relaxed purpose and pace of the day centre.

In the town, in contrast, there were a number of instances of inter-agency conflict, some of which stemmed from the lack of choice. Although both psychogeriatric day hospitals and Part III day centres offered day care, both aimed for a high quality intensive regime which did not suit those more in need of essentially recreational care. As a result clients did not always get the service they needed. The shortcomings of day care are compounded by the limitations of some of the domiciliary services, for example the restricted home care service and the absence of a sitting service. Case 009, a single man of 79 quoted earlier as an example of successful co-ordinated care in the community, illustrated this conflict near the end of his life.

> He had been attending the Part III Day Centre
> for several years, but following referral to
> the psychogeriatrician attended the Day
> Hospital for 3 days a week for reality
> orientation and physical treatment. Later he
> reverted to 5 days at the Part III Day Centre
> as he was suitably placed there and presented
> no management problems (in the view of the
> Day Hospital staff) and did not like going to
> the Day Hospital which had not helped him
> (in the view of the Part III Day Centre
> staff).

Case 010, a widow of 86 is another about whom perceptions differ.

> At the beginning of the study period she had
> been attending the psychogeriatric day
> hospital, with one week in four in a short-
> term care bed in the psychogeriatric ward.
> She was then accepted on a trial basis for 2
> days a week at the Part III Day Centre, and
> four months later her day care remained
> divided between the two, although her
> dementia was so great, and her social skills
> so diminished, that neither felt she was
> appropriately placed with them. The officer
> in charge of day care felt that day care (at
> least in its available varieties) was not the
> right place for her: 'She gets nothing from
> coming here, though her daughter (the carer)
> does. On account of her presence I may have
> to turn down someone for whom day care would
> be a benefit'. The daughter, who had been
> caring for several years since her mother had
> had a stroke, was reported to be in favour of
> her mother going into hospital.

The lack of choice in the town may account in part for the lack of consensus in what kind of additional day care provision is needed, as has been described in Chapter Five. While there are undoubtedly instances where an individual would benefit from 'Seven Day a Week' day care, these appear relatively few and far between, and apply only during brief periods of an individual's dementia career. Such needs could often be met by an extension of domiciliary services.

6.7 Residential care

Over three-quarters of the sample have had experience since they began to dement with some kind of residential care. Nearly two-thirds of those with such experience were already permanent residents (see Table 6.6). Use of residential care was especially heavy among the town sample.

Table 6.6 Use of Residential Care

	No	None	Short-term only	Temporary-subsequently permanent	Permanent only
City	56	18	15	14	9
Town	44	6	14	14	10

Experience of temporary residential care had been in psychogeriatric hospital wards (18), geriatric wards (11) and a very wide range of other hospital provision; and in ordinary Part III homes (14) and a number of other forms of non-hospital accommodation. Of those who had gone into residential care permanently, 17 had been exclusively in hospital, 19 in institutions other than hospitals, and 11 in both hospitals and non-hospitals. Of the 24 with no experience of residential care, two had short-term care planned, and in four other cases the eventuality had been discussed. Much short-term care was by planned admissions to give relief to relatives; these generally worked well, once any initial problems of acceptability to patients and carers had been overcome.

The difficulties experienced by the sample can be grouped as follows: achieving entry into residential care, choosing the right establishment, difficulties of management, and problems of transfer and discharge.

There was considerable evidence of refusal of residential care by people whose workers felt this to be an appropriate solution to their problems. These included both candidates for short-term care (five in various settings) and permanent care (three refusals of Part III). Three others entered Part III only after some delay and a lot of persuasion. In several cases, the subject's or the carer's fear of the psychiatric hospital (due to its reputation) prevented or delayed admission to its psychogeriatric wards.

In 14 cases there was a degree of difficulty in choosing and obtaining a suitable kind of residential care. Three were relatively minor and straightforward, three were major conflicts within the health service; three conflicts between health and social services and five were searches within the private sector.

Seventeen subjects had presented difficulties of management due to their behaviour while in residential care. Five settled after initial difficulties in Part III and three others had difficult but contained short-term care in Part III. Most of the other difficulties concerned behaviour in private residential homes or in nursing homes, which led generally to admission to psychiatric hospital. Three other cases presented difficulties over medication regimes.

The ideal integration of day care and residential services has not always been possible to achieve. One resident in a private residential home would have benefitted from the stimulation of day care, but this was not being provided. She was not disabled enough to warrant a place in a day hospital or local authority day care scheme, and the voluntary day centre was provided for those whose relatives would benefit from their attending; people in residential care were generally excluded. In two other cases, the proprietor of a private residential home considered his residents were suffering greater confusion, not less, as a result of attending day hospital, and he considered that both benefitted when he was able to arrange for them to stop attending.

Three cases emerged where transfer from one kind of residential care to another created difficulties for the services. One of these (066, who took a lot of persuading to move from a community hospital to a psychogeriatric ward in a psychiatric hospital) has already been described. A second was unresolved after a five month wait.

> Case 060. A widow of 88 who had been living in Part III homes since 1980. The Oic considered her dementia was worsening, but as she was a much-loved resident, and presented no behaviour problems (although she needed a wheelchair and assistance in all tasks) he delayed referral to a psychogeriatrician for six months. The consultant visited, and put her on a waiting list for a long-stay bed; but the situation five months later was unchanged.

And a third produced improvement with a less than ideal solution.

> Case 001. A widow of 72 experienced considerable mental distress as a result of a conflict among the relatives with whom she was living. She was admitted as an emergency to Part III and after a nervous start, settled in well. After six months, the social worker attempted to move her to a more independent 'part-care' scheme. The Oic admits she is capable of more independent living, but feels she still needs the security of Part III. She wants her to stay as 'she is an asset to the home'.

Some examples of difficulties at discharge due to problems over medication have already been noted. In another nine cases there were serious problems for other reasons. In four cases subjects were discharged home out of residential care at the insistence of relatives (three husbands and a brother). In two of the cases, readmission was needed on the same day. In another discharge took place against the relatives' wishes: they called the GP who got her readmitted immediately.

In several other cases, there were major failures of communication between services. Two were discharged from psychiatric hospitals without the home care service being informed. Two others produced more serious crises. One, Case 044, has been described earlier:

> Taken home from psychiatric hospital on a day assessment by a local authority social worker. But electricity and water had not been reconnected and the day was wasted. This episode precipitated a crisis meeting between community and ward staff to establish lines of contact.

> Case 037. The husband of this dementing 86-year old was in a community hospital. She was admitted to another hospital with Parkinson's disease. The husband was more competent mentally but had a potentially fatal heart condition. She was transferred to his hospital to be near him. He improved and was discharged. The geriatrician considered that as she was

mobile she was not a geriatric case. The psychogeriatrician felt she was primarily a social problem and fit for Part III. The local authority social worker was unable to persuade her to enter Part III, so that for a time she remained in hospital in a GP bed. The home situation was fraught with the husband liable to die at any moment: the daughter and her husband (who lived next door) solicitous that the old man's last days should be as peaceful as possible, and the daughter threatening to leave home if her mother returned.

The hospital social worker pleaded with the GP to keep her in a little longer, but he took the view, 'There was no medical reason to keep her in, and I wanted the bed, so I had to precipitate a crisis in social services ...... she was their responsibility ...... I had asked the geriatrician and the psychogeriatrician, neither of whom considered her a candidate for their hospital beds. I was pressured for beds. She wanted to go home'.

She was discharged on a Saturday. Within hours, the daughter had contacted the duty GP who referred on to the Emergency Duty Team of the SSD. Later that day she was persuaded to enter the local Part III home, which happened to have a vacancy. In the month following her admission she settled in well.

In contrast to such problems, there were several instances when entry into residential care was quickly arranged and smoothly and successfully executed.

Case 095. A single lady of 84, who was admitted to a Part III home within two months of being referred to the SSD by her GP. Factors contributing to the successful resolution of her application appeared to be (i) an appropriate referral by the GP (ii) the subject in good physical health and able to articulate her needs (iii) caring and sensible relatives (iv) prompt offer of a place in a suitable home (v) appropriate handling by SSD staff.

Other successful examples concerned entry into private homes: two into a home whose proprietor specifically welcomes dementing residents, and two into a home run on *laissez-faire* lines, whose welcome stretched to including residents' pets. As one of the sample insisted on being accompanied into residential care by two cats and a large dog, this was a particularly useful option.

Discharge from hospital proved a particularly problematic time for services to act in unison. One discharge provides therefore a welcome contrast with some of the stories recounted elsewhere.

> Case 083. A married woman of 83 was admitted to a geriatrician's bed for assessment. Her husband was frail, and after some five weeks, the hospital social worker asked the SSD to consider them for Part III. The SSD staff were alarmed, as they knew the consultant was on holiday and had not made a full assessment. They persuaded the hospital to keep her. The consultant returned two weeks later and diagnosed dyskynesia, incontinence, mild dementia, difficult personality and stiffness with unwillingness to move! She improved and was soon ready for discharge, but the consultant kept her a further five weeks until an appropriate Part III place became available.

6.8 Service refusal

One theme which recurred over and over again during the reconstruction of dementia careers was that of service refusal. About half of the sample had at some stage refused (either personally or through their carers) a service which the service givers had wished to provide. Altogether 19 refused residential care of one sort or another, 16 refused day care, 12 refused home helps, and a wide spectrum of other assistance was also declined. Table 6.7 gives the details.

Table 6.7 Services declined by subject or carer

		City	Town
Residential Services:			
	Part III	2	6
	Private home	2	0
	Short-term care	2	4
	Sheltered housing	1	1
	Hospital	1	0
		8	11
Day Care:			
	Day hospital	4	4
	LA day centre	4	1
	Voluntary DC	3	0
		11	5
Home help		7	5
Meals-on-Wheels		4	1
Psychiatric referral		1	2
Other service		6	0

6.9 Summary

This chapter has described the experiences of 100 demented elderly people, in terms of their service contacts, seen through the eyes of the workers providing their service help. A series of patterns of service use, and difficulties facing service providers have emerged.

1. The timing of the initial onset is often poorly acknowledged and recorded. GPs face difficulties with patients in the early stages of dementia. What should the GP (or other workers, if they are the first to suspect dementia) do? To whom should they refer, and when? Some cases show conflicts among domiciliary care providers, although there are some success stories.

2. The two SSDs in the study showed contrasting approaches in their handling of demented clients at home.

3. The work of the psychogeriatric service would have benefitted from an open referral system.

Prior referral to another medical specialism, or good physical health of the patient, could often delay referral. A well-developed CPN service appeared particularly valuable.

4. The use of day services was widespread, although for many demented elderly attendance had been brief and/or disastrous. A choice of day care regimes was very valuable.

5. Most of the sample had had experience of residential care in either hospital or residential home. Short-term care usually appeared successful in the workers' views. Difficulties concerned achieving entry, choosing the right establishment, difficulties of management, and problems of transfer and discharge.

6. Service refusal by the patient or carer was a familiar theme: half of the sample had refused a service that service personnel wanted to provide, and the entire spectrum of provision was included.

7 BRINGING THE RESEARCH TOGETHER

What do the research exercises described in the previous two chapters tell us about the way services are provided for demented elderly people? How do the services in the two locations under scrutiny compare with examples of good and bad practice elsewhere?

Identification and initial management of dementia

The little data available from this study on the initial recognition of dementia confirms other research that there is poor agreement between relatives and GPs on the date of onset; there is usually an appreciable gap between relatives detecting that something is wrong and taking action, and clinicians at least at primary care level, are not expert in predicting which dementias will develop.

Dementia often remains difficult to diagnose with precision. Yet it remains worth attempting. Jorm (1987) describes the advantages of early and accurate diagnosis conferring reassurance for the relatives, and a greater likelihood that medication will be correctly matched with medical need.

Despite the growing resources of the psychogeriatric service in both locations, referrals to it are not made particularly early, although the great majority appear to be appropriate. GPs in the urban area are increasingly able to distinguish (and to indicate in their letter of referral) whether the initial visit to the patient should be made by a psychogeriatrician or a CPN, plus an indication of the appropriate degree of urgency. But many GPs still need further guidance on the matter, possibly including being told of the range of services available, which is so varied from one place to another, and which is constantly changing.

Dementing people are often referred by GPs to geriatricians initially, to exclude possible organic causes of the dementia. While this is desirable, care must be taken to ensure that such procedures do not unduly delay referral to the psychogeriatrician, when this also seems appropriate. There is also a danger that dementing elderly people who remain physically healthy are not referred to a psychogeriatrician as promptly as appropriate.

SSDs face problems in providing appropriate domiciliary services. This is especially true to the crucial home care service. Firstly, especially in the rural area, the element of financial cost deters some potential clients. Home care organizers sometimes need all their powers of persuasion to win clients' acceptability for a service they consider is self-evidently necessary. Reducing the financial cost to users would therefore help the service to be applied where it could be most beneficial; removing it altogether would have the additional benefit of making its administration simpler. There is however some opinion that services paid for by clients are more valued by them.

Secondly, allocation procedures, especially in the urban area, direct the great majority of referrals to either 'home care' or 'social care' teams. Thus dementing clients (or their carers) who might benefit from the help of a trained social worker could find this subsequently hard to obtain. They may become 'trapped' among the clientele of the home care service. Home helps receive little training, and as such are ill-equipped to identify dementia.

Third, the home care service remains a largely five-day office-hours service; at times it relies on the goodwill of its staff for effective working with dementing elderly clients. Sometimes (e.g. Case 035 discussed in Chapter Six) a flexible approach by the home help has been extremely beneficial to the client, and ultimately to the whole caring service apparatus, by keeping a client at home and out of residential care. Other domiciliary services appeared to be working reasonably well, although there were examples of conflict and lack of co-operation between them.

Most of these conflicts concerned relations between the CPN service and local authority social workers in the rural area. Some of these concerned admission to Part III homes and discharges from hospital. In the urban area, in contrast, these two services appeared to make little contact with one another. This may have come about due to the development of the psychogeriatric service, embracing both CPNs and its own social workers, who appeared to deal actively with a large caseload, many of whom were living at home. The caseload of the SSD social workers was thus restricted, and appeared to contain a large number of cases whose problems were relatively intractable, and who were unlikely to be presented as straightforward dementia cases.

The task for social workers in these cases - what they should actually be trying to *do* - is not often easy, and usually far removed from conventional case-work. Both SSDs confirmed the impression of Coleman *et al.*, (1982, p.66):

> Social work counselling, which one might imagine would be an important role for qualified social workers with dementing elderly people and their families, was not strongly evident and did not seem to be perceived as important by other professionals.

There were several cases who formed spectacular exceptions to this generalization. Case 001, for example, was a widow of 72 who lived in a conflict-torn household with younger relatives. Despite all the social worker's attempts at help, her health deteriorated (probably due more to stress than dementia) and she was admitted as an emergency to a Part III home, where she settled in well. Other cases (059 and 076 described earlier) illustrated family conflict which was successfully handled through intensive intervention. That this was achieved by a CPN rather than a social worker was largely coincidental.

The lower-than-expected number of patients identified by domiciliary services in both locations suggests that screening would be a valuable exercise to uncover cases where service help could be usefully offered. Yet the workers interviewed in this research were with the exception of two health visitors opposed to the idea, on pragmatic grounds. Two GPs in the city had tried to do some, but without apparent success. A rural GP considered it a threat to job satisfaction. A rural health visitor echoed these sentiments: she worked with a single-handed GP, and reckoned her role would be reduced if she had to do screening visits. A nurse manager disapproved of screening on the grounds of cost; a DHA estimate calculated 15 additional HVs would be needed if all over-75s were visited annually. However, the attempt to mobilize volunteers to perform routine visits to elderly patients on behalf of the primary health team (Beales and Hicks, 1988) which was described briefly in Chapter Three, took place in a very similar location to the town described in this report, and appears an excellent example of mobilizing one section of the population (most of the volunteers were fit people around retirement age) to assist another, more vulnerable group.

Day care

The problems of day care have been spelt out clearly: the need to provide a sufficient choice in day care, and to engage and retain clients. Eight of the sample of 100 dementia sufferers refused to attend, and another 15 attended only briefly. In addition there are obvious difficulties in providing day care (and especially transport) for scattered rural populations. Day care remains an area where the voluntary sector can provide an invaluable component of the service, enabling day hospitals and more theraputically-oriented day centres (provided for example by the local authority) to fulfil their potential. The two areas of field-work provided vividly contrasting examples of success and failure in this endeavour.

Residential care

Various areas of difficulty appear in dealing with dementia in residential care.

Entry itself was not always straightforward. Dementia may already be a problem, as it was with two of this sample, and 17% of the sample of 167 elderly people admitted to private residential care (Challis and Day, 1982). Allocation practice often chose those living in the community, against those who were 'inappropriately placed but safe' (e.g. in a psychiatric hospital). While this lessened the burden of emotional risk borne by workers, and physical risk borne by clients, it meant that other institutions faced periods of inefficiency, enduring clients whose needs now lay elsewhere. Case 060, waiting five months in a Part III home for a psychogeriatric bed, is a case in point. Elsewhere, the scale of 'bed blockage' may be enormous: in July 1986 almost ten per cent of the 1200 acute beds in Camberwell were occupied by elderly patients awaiting discharge, mostly because of accommodation requirements (Ham, 1988).

Despite the pressure on places almost constantly in all types of residential provision, there was little evidence that patients were 'bounced around'. Swaps between institutions occurred occasionally. But there were numerous instances where discharge from residential care was a time fraught with difficulties for the patient. These instances appeared to have little in common beyond a failure to communicate among components of the service network at that moment.

Services in contrasting areas

Many differences in service mix and service performance are apparent from this study, beyond the crude distinction between urban and rural. Some can be put down to history, some to personal idiosyncracy. For example, GP beds were available only in the rural area. While these were valued resources, they were not without problems, (e.g. at the time of patient discharge). *The Rising Tide*'s assertion that 'the principal division that affects the organization of services is that between town and country' (HAS, 1982, p.22) may be true, but many other factors are likely to influence how services dealing with any area are organized.

Other themes appeared from the research powerfully but impressionistically: that of service refusal by patients and carers; the value of a key worker; the need for more education about dementia among the whole spectrum of workers.

Service refusal was dealt with at length in Chapter Six. The concept of key worker was not used widely in the areas covered by this research, and while it has undoubtedly value in orchestrating service input for some dependent people, it is not without problems. Addison (1986) for example, describes two cases where a social worker took on the role, although fellow-workers outside the social service departments did not necessarily share the view that the social worker held that role. In one or two of the cases described in Chapter Six, it seemed that for practical purposes it was the nearest neighbour who performed that role.

Educational needs were described briefly in Chapter Five. Certainly both research exercises confirmed the concern that those whose primary task lay not with dementia (nurses in non-psychiatric settings, staff in Part III and private residential homes, home helps and others) were short on the skills needed to identify and handle elderly people with dementia. The value of education has been widely endorsed elsewhere (Smyer and Gatz, 1983; Astrom, 1986) but attempts to promote positive attitudes towards the elderly among medical workers and students have had only limited success (Coccaro and Miles, 1984).

8 SUMMING UP

How typical is this study nationally?

Variations locally in the scope, availability and range of service provision for dementing old people are certainly huge. As services develop and become more complex, they are unlikely to be provided evenly throughout the country. The most urgent needs in one place are unlikely to be the same as those in another. How typical is the situation reported here?

First, aspects of the local population and economy must be emphasized. Both areas studied were reasonably affluent. This was particularly important with respect to the residential sector; there were plenty of private homes in the area, although few appeared able to take new residents without some time on a waiting list. Some dementia sufferers who could not afford to pay were able to get into private homes with the assistance of DHSS funds. Access to the private sector clearly offered greater choice: an example was that one private home took pets. For the statutory services, probably the greatest beneficiaries of the consequent reduction in the number of those desiring admission were the local authority's Part III homes.

Secondly, the contribution of the voluntary sector appears to be idiosyncratic. It made a valuable contribution to the lives of dementing old people in the city, but very little impact in the rural area. There appears to be no explanation for this difference other than the activities of a handful of individuals in the city, who saw a need and instigated and organized a response. The use of volunteers to carry out a screening or befriending role is a recent innovation described in earlier chapters which needs leadership from within existing services, notably primary care teams. The organization of volunteer help in this way is still rare, calling for leadership from existing services.

Thirdly, the research programme did not permit any investigation of services for dementing old people in metropolitan conurbations, or in rural areas comprising scattered villages and a low density of human settlement. Most studies of the prevalence of dementia have been conducted, as shown in Chapter Two, in urban areas, often in big cities. Such locations may contain a high proportion of elderly people who are isolated from all kin contact, and possibly therefore more vulnerable to dementia. The wider consideration of social class in dementia remains virtually ignored by researchers. The importance of housing is obvious: an isolated demented old person may cope in a rural cottage, given basic support from neighbours and appropriate services; in a high-rise block such a person may rapidly become a threat to others, for example through leaving gas supplies on and unlit. Genuinely rural areas are also likely to pose particular problems through the difficulties of supplying service help to scattered individual clients. Finally, the pace of change in the manner services are provided is considerable. Demands are changing too. Flexibility, adaptability and fresh thinking will clearly be needed for some time to come. As Challis and Davies (1980, p.1) sum up,

> 'It has become clear that we shall not
> be able to cope with the increasing and
> changing needs of the elderly using the
> same mix of services as we have during
> the early 1970s. Need is growing
> faster than resources, and the pattern
> of need is itself changing'.

Lessons for the NHS

Several weaknesses in the system have been identified. The need to co-ordinate services carefully at the point of hospital discharge was shown up by several cases already quoted.

There is a need to promote a more positive awareness of dementia and sources of help (as distinct from treatment regimes) among GPs. Although the two practices used in this research were chosen as they had volunteered for collaboration (and may therefore be assumed to have an above-average awareness of dementia) they found it difficult to bring to mind more than a small proportion of their patients suffering from dementia that community surveys would expect them to have. In this respect, they followed a familiar pattern. Above all, GPs need to be alert to options other than referral to a psychogeriatrician.

Finally, several cases illustrated the need for an open referral system. Usually this came about through a social worker wanting a psychogeriatric referral, but being unable to get the GP to set it in motion. In one case the social worker saw the GP as the only route into the psychogeriatric service. In another, the patient's son shared this wish, but the GP took the view, 'I've cured the patient before and I'll cure her again'. In another case the Oic in a Part III home wanted a psychiatric referral but the GP blocked it. In several other cases it was a relative (usually the patient's husband) who resisted referral.

Lessons for SSDs

Several clear messages for Social Service Departments arise out of this research, spanning the spectrum of their service provision. Residential provision in Part III homes involves providing for an increasingly demented clientele, although the organization of services as yet takes little account of this fact. In the city, the specialist EMI home went some way to filling this large gap, but provision for those residents suffering from dementia in the SSD's other homes was far from ideal. Transfer of residents from Part III homes to hospital was sometimes subject to considerable delay. In the town, the situation was rather worse, with no specialist provision. Yet a new home opened in the town nearest to the study town in the course of the field work, and initial impressions suggested that many of the first wave of residents were demented, and that they were cared for well in the initial stages. Since the field-work was completed, research elsewhere reveals a large number of dementing residents and an inappropriately trained body of staff (Ineichen, in preparation).

Field-work staff also need careful attention. In the city, the flourishing CPN service meant that many of the clients left residually on the SSD's books suffered dementia-like symptoms often as concomitant to intractable social problems. In the circumstances, field social workers faced an uphill battle. The home care service, given good resources and with high morale, performed well, although the minimal training the home helps received remained an enduring source of concern.

In the town, field-work services were offered differently. Many cases were dealt with by social work assistants with good day care and residential back up, the service generally worked well. However, relations with health service agencies were full of conflict: over appropriate day care, for example (which clients should go to day care in the Part III homes, and which in the day hospital?) and over the organization of care for discharged hospital patients. The scarcity of CPN resources may have been a major contributory factor in this.

Both SSDs were accused of slowness of response to referrals; their working must seem cumbersome to outsiders, and they lacked a sophisticated scheme for grading the urgency of their referrals.

Lessons for the voluntary sector

The two areas under scrutiny provided a sharp contrast when the voluntary sector was considered. No explanation appears possible for this other than by underlining the role taken by a handful of influential and energetic individuals in the city. The key to the success of these individuals lies in their apparent ability to collaborate, rather than compete, with statutory services.

Arie (1984) sounds a warning here. While the consumer voice is an essential ingredient in planning new services, it must be treated with caution as far as long-term residential care is concerned: what is heard is not the voices of residents, but those of the relatives who put them there.

Towards integrated provision

As with the voluntary sector, the role of key innovative individuals throughout the whole spectrum of services was noted in *The Rising Tide* (HAS, 1982, p.25) and has been confirmed here. Consultant psychogeriatricians have considerably more scope to innovate than any equivalent personnel in Social Services.

However, much can usefully be done at organizational level. Wasteful conflict, such as that between NHS and SSD day care agencies in the town for the same group of clients can be avoided. Small sums of money involved in developing voluntary agencies can be used to test out innovative ideas. Research can be used, as in this study, to explore gaps in service provision where responsibility fails to fall neatly to a particular agency.

Public awareness

However, some tasks remain still beyond the remit of anyone engaged in the existing service network. The need for further education of many professional groups is clear from the views and the experiences of workers and sufferers described in these pages. Yet a further task remains: that of educating the public.

As the authors of *The Rising Tide* have pointed out (HAS, 1982, p. 27) there is a need to raise expectations if what is in places a very bad service is ever to improve. Public awareness of what dementia is, and what can be done about it, also needs attention. The author has recently been involved with a street survey on public attitudes to mental illness in Newham, East London. Two thirds of those asked, 'Would you go to your doctor if you had an elderly relative living alone near your home, who was not looking after herself?' said they would go to their doctor, but in many cases this was to obtain a referral to a more appropriate agency. There was virtually no awareness among the 175 people questioned that such a situation could arise as a result of a physical, treatable illness. A greater willingness to discuss dementia openly should lead to a more effective response by those who can help.

As Cutler (1986) has pointed out, stigma attached to mental illness may lead some people to separate dementia from other forms of mental illness, inhibiting the help-seeking process. This may be especially true of older people. The views of relatives may differ significantly from workers, not only in respect of what dementia is, but of what should be done about their dementing relative. A generation which has seen institutionalization, being 'put away' as the only solution, may well look askance at less drastic methods of management.

It is well to end on a note of hope. Cutler (1986) has given an account of the spectacular rise of the ADRDA (Alzheimer's Disease and Related Disorders Association) in the U.S.A. Within a few days of its office opening in 1980, they received 25,000 letters although they only had one member of staff. It is not unreasonable to assume that most were from carers unsatisfied at what help they had found available. Organizations in Britain like the Alzheimer's Disease Society and Scottish Action on Dementia have begun to harness the huge volume of concern that exists around dementia and create a much better-informed and more actively involved public. Many other local groups add to this process. The result will undoubtedly be pressure too on the statutory services to provide more effective, comprehensive and local services.

ABBREVIATIONS

CHC	-	Community Health Council
CPN	-	Community psychiatric nurse
DHA	-	District Health Authority
DHSS	-	Department of Health and Social Security
DNS	-	district nursing sister
EMI	-	elderly mentally infirm
EPH	-	elderly persons' home
GP	-	general (medical) practitioner
HAS	-	Health Advisory Service
HV	-	health visitor
LASW	-	local authority social worker
MID	-	multi-infarct dementia
MSW	-	medical social worker
NHS	-	National Health Service
Oic	-	Officer-in-charge (of old peoples' home)
OT	-	occupational therapist
Part III home	-	local authority home for elderly people
RHA	-	Regional Health Authority
SDAT	-	Senile Dementia of the Alzheimer Type
SSD	-	Social Services Department
SWA	-	social work assistant

REFERENCES

Addison, C. (1986) The wish to stay at home. *Social Work Today*, **11** August, 10-11.

Allen, I. (1983) *Short-stay residential care for the elderly*, Policy Studies Institute.

Ames, D., Ashby, D., Mann, A.H. and Graham, N. (1988) Psychiatric illness in elderly residents of Part III homes in one London borough: prognosis and review. *Age and Ageing*, **17**, 249-56.

Arie, T. (1983) Organisation of services for the elderly: implications for education and patient care. Experience in Nottingham. In *Geropsychiatric Diagnostics and Treatment* (ed M. Berenger), Springer, 189-95.

Arie, T. (1984) Don't play pass the parcel with the demented. *Geriatric Medicine*, July/Aug, p.9-11.

Arie, T. (1986) Some current issues in old age psychiatry services. In *The Provision of Mental Health Services in Britain: The way ahead*(eds. G. Wilkinson and H. Freeman), Gaskell 79-88.

Arie, T. and Jolley, D. (1982) Making services work: Organisation and style of psychogeriatric services. In *The Psychiatry of Late Life* (eds. R. Levy and F. Post), Blackwell, 222-51.

Askham, J., Lindesay, J., Murphy, D., Rapley, C. and Thompson, C. (1987) *Enhanced Home Support for Dementia Sufferers*, Age Concern /Institute of Gerontology.

Astrom, S. (1986) Health care students attitudes towards, and intention to work with patients suffering from senile dementia. *J. Advanced Nursing*, **11**, 651-9.

Barley, S. (1987) An uncompromising report on health visiting for the elderly. *Br. Med. J.*, **294**, 595-6.

Barnes, R.F., Raskind, M.A., Scott, M. and Murphy, C. (1981) Problems of families caring for Alzheimer patients; use of a support group. *J. A. Geriatrics Society*, **29**, 80-85.

Beales, D. and Hicks, E. (1988) Volunteers help to detect unreported medical problems in the elderly. *The Practitioner*, **232**, 478-82.

Bergmann, K. (1985) Epidemiological aspects of dementia and

considerations in planning services. *Danish Medical Bulletin*, **32** (Supp. 1) ,84-91.

Bergmann K. and Jacoby, R. (1983) The limitations and possibilities for community care for the elderly demented. In D.H.S.S. *Elderly People in the Community, their Service Needs*, H.M.S.O.

Bergmann, K., Foster, E.M., Justice, A.W. and Mathews, V. (1978) Management of the elderly demented patient in the community. *B. J. Psychiatry*, **132**, 441-9.

Bergmann, K., Manchee, V. and Woods, R.T. (1984) Effects of family relationships on psychogeriatric patients. *J. Roy. Soc. Med.*, **77**, 840-4.

Bergmann, K., Proctor, S. and Prudham, D. (1979) Symptom profiles in hospital and community resident elderly persons with dementia. In Bayer-Symposium 7, *Brain Function in Old Age*, Springer Verlag, Heidelberg.

Black, J. (1985) *Care Network Project*, Working Paper 37, University College of North Wales.

Blessed, G. and Wilson, I. D. (1982) The contemporary natural history of mental disorder in old age. *B. J. Psychiatry*, **141**, 59-67.

Bollerup, T.R. (1975) Prevalence of mental illness among 70 year-olds domiciled in nine Copenhagen suburbs. *Acta Psychiatrica Scandinavia*, **51**, 327-39.

Bond, J. (1987) Psychiatric illness in later life: a study of prevalence in a Scottish population. *I.J. Geriatric Psychiatry*, **2**, (1), 39-57.

Booth, T.A. (1978) From normal baby to handicapped child: unravelling the idea of subnormality in families of mentally handicapped children. *Sociology*, **12**, (2), 203-21.

Broe, G.A., Akhtar, A.J., Andrews, G.R., Caird, F.I., Gilmore, A.J.J. and McLennan, W.J. (1976) Neurological diagnosis in the elderly at home. *J. Neurology, Neurosurgery and Psychiatry*, **39**, 362-66.

Bruce, N. (1980) *Teamwork for Preventive Care*, Research Studies Press.

Burns, B.J., Larson, D.B., Goldstrom, I.D., Johnson, W.E., Taube, C.A., Miller, N.E. and Mathis E.S. (1988) Mental Disorder among nursing home patients: preliminary findings from the national nursing home survey protest. *I. J. Geriatric Psychiatry*, **3**, 27-35.

Campbell, A.J., McCosh, L.M., Reinken, J.and Allan, B.C. (1983) Dementia in old age and the need for services. *Age and Ageing*, **12**, 11-16.

Cantley, C. and Hunter, D. (1985) People processing: a typology of selected GP referral and admission practices in the case of elderly people. *Ageing and Society*, **5**, (3), 267-88.

Carter, J. (1981) *Day Services for Adults: Somewhere to go*, Allen and Unwin.

Challis, D. and Davies, B. (1980) A new approach to community care for the elderly. *B. J. Social Work*, **10**, 1-18.

Challis, D. and Davies, B. (1986) *Case Management in Community Care*, Gower.

Challis, L. and Day, P. (1982) *Private and Voluntary Residential Provision for the Elderly*, Centre for Analysis of Social Policy, University of Bath.

Christie, A. B. (1982) Changing patterns in mental illness in the elderly. *B. J. Psychiatry*, **140**, 154-9.

Christie, A. B. (1985) Survival in dementia: a review in *Recent Advances in Psychogeriatrics I* (ed. T. Arie), Churchill Livingstone.

Christie, A. B. and Train, J. D. (1984) Changes in the pattern of care for the demented. *B. J. Psychiatry*, **144**, 9-15.

Clarke, M., Lowry R. and Clarke S., (1986) Cognitive impairment in the elderly: a community survey. *Age and Ageing*, **15**, 278-284.

Coccaro, E. F. and Miles, A. M. (1984) The attitudinal impact of training in gerontology/geriatrics in medical school. *J. A. Geriatrics Soc.*, **32**, (10), 762-8.

Coleman, P. *et al* (1982) *Collaboration Between Services for the Elderly Mentally Infirm*, Dept. of Social Work Studies and Faculty of Medicine (Geriatric Medicine), University of Southampton.

Cooper, B. (1984) Home and away: the disposition of mentally ill old people in an urban population. *Social Psychiatry*, **19**, 187-96.

Cooper, B. (1987) Psychiatric disorders among elderly patients admitted to hospital medical wards. *J. Roy. Soc. Med.*, **80**, (1), 13-16.

Cooper, B. and Bickel, H. (1984) Population screening and the early detection of dementing disorders in old age, a review. *Psychological Medicine*, **14**, 81-95.

Cooper, B. and Sosna, U. (1983) Psychische erkrankung in der alterberolberung, eine epidemilogische feltstudie in Mannheim. *Nervenartzt*, **54**, 239-49.

Copeland, J.R.M., Dewey, M.E., Wood, N., Searle, R., Davidson, I.A. and McWilliam, C. (1987) Range of mental illness among the elderly in the community: Prevalence in Liverpool using the GMS. AGECAT Package. *B.J. Psychiatry*, **150**, 815-23.

Crosby, C., Stevenson, R.C. and Copeland, J.R.M. (1984) The evaluation of intensive domiciliary care for the elderly mentally ill. In *Gerontology : Social and Behavioural Aspects* (ed. D.B. Bromley), Croom Helm, 79-87

References

Cutler, N.E. (1986) Public Response: the national politics of Alzheimer's disease. In *The Dementias: Policy and Management* (eds. M.L.M. Gilhooly, S.H. Zarit and J.E. Birren), Prentice Hall Englewood Cliffs, pp.161-89.

D'Alessandro, R., Gallassi, R., Benassi, G., Morreale, A. and Lugaresi, E. (1988) Dementia in subjects over 65 years of age in the Republic of San Marino. *B. J. Psychiatry*, **153**, 182-6.

Dalziel, M. and Richards, K. (1987) Community based incontinence services in a health authority. *Community Medicine*, **9**, (4), 359-64.

Davies, B. and Challis, D. (1986) *Matching Resources to Needs in Community Care*, Gower.

Dexter,M. and Harbert,W. (1983) *The Home Help Service*, Tavistock.

Diesfeldt, H.F.A. (1986) Duration of survival in dementia. *Acta Psychiatrica Scandinavia*, **73**, 366-71.

Dowd, J. J. (1984) Mental illness and the aged stranger, *I. J. Health Services*, **14**, 1.

Doyle, B. and Hunt, P. (1985) Day care for the elderly. *Health and Social Service Journal*, 11 April, 448-9.

Eagles, J.M., Craig, A., Rawlinson, F., Restall, D.B., Beattie, J.A.G. and Besson, J.A.O. (1987a), The psychological well-being of supporters of the demented elderly. *B. J. Psychiatry*, **150**, 293-8.

Eagles, J.M., Beattie, J.A.G., Blackwood, G.W., Restall D.B., and Ashcroft, G.W. (1987b) The mental health of elderly couples I The effects of a cognitively impaired spouse. *B. J. Psychiatry*, **150**, 299-303.

Evans, N., Kendal, I., Lovelock, R. and Powell, J. (1986) Something to look forward to: an evaluation of a travelling day hospital for elderly mentally ill people. SSRIU, Portsmouth Poly and Hampshire SSD.

Fenton, T.W. (1987) AIDS - related Psychiatric Disorder. *B.J. Psychiatry*, **157**, 579-88.

Folstein, M.A., Anthony, J.C., Parhad, I., Duffy, B. and Grunenberg, E.M. (1985) The meaning of cognitive impairment in the elderly. *J. A. Geriatrics Soc.*, **33**, 228-35.

Fox, P. (1988) Group life for the elderly mentally ill. *Geriatric Nursing and Home Care*, **8**, (1), 24-5.

Francis, W. (1986) Great promise. *Community Care*, 13 March, 17-19.

Fraser, M. (1987) *Dementia: its nature and management*, Wiley.

Fraser, R.M. and Healey, R. (1986) Psychogeriatric liaison: a service to a district general hospital. *Bulletin R. College Psychiatrists*, **10**, 312-14.

Fry, J. (1984) Checking on the elderly: should we bother? *Update*, 15 December.

George, L.K. and Gwyther, L.P. (1986) Caregiver well being: a multi-dimensional examination of family caregivers of demented adults. *Gerontologist*, **26**, 253-9.

Gilhooly, M. L. M. (1984) The social dimensions of senile dementia. In *Psychological Approaches to the Care of the Elderly* (eds. I. Hanley and J Hodge), Croom Helm. pp.88-135.

Gilhooly, M. L. M. (1986) Senile dementia: Factors associated with caregivers' preference for institutional care. *B. J. Medical Psychology*, **59**, 165-71.

Gilleard, C. J. (1984) *Living with Dementia*, Croom Helm

Gilleard, C. J. (1985) The psychogeriatric patient and his family. In *Research Highlights in Social Work II; Responding to Mental Illness* (ed. G. Horobin), Kogan Page, pp.43-55.

Gilleard, C. J. (1987) Influence of emotional distress among supporters on the outcome of psychogeriatric day care. *B. J. Psychiatry*, **150**, 219-23.

Gilmore, A.J.J. (1977) Brain failure at home. *Age and Ageing*, **6** (Suppl.), 56-60.

Godber, C. (1978) Conflict and collaboartion between geriatric medicine and psychiatry In *Recent Advances in Geriatric Medicine* (ed. B. Isaacs), Churchill Livingstone, pp.131-42.

Godber, C. (1987) Psychogeriatric and social services for the demented. In *Dementia* (ed. B. Pitt), Churchill Livingstone, pp.296-316.

Gruer, R. (1975) *Needs of the Elderly in the Scottish Borders*, Scottish Home and Health Department.

Grundy, E. (1987) Community care of the elderly 1976-84. *Br. Med. J.*, **294**, 626-9.

Grundy, E. and Arie, T. (1982) Falling rate of provision of residential care for the elderly. *Br. Med. J.*, **284**, 779-802.

Grundy, E. and Arie, T. (1984) Institutionalisation and the elderly: international comparison. *Age and Ageing*, **13**, 129-37.

Gubrium, J. F. (1988) Family responsibility and care giving for Alzheimer's disease victims. *J. Marriage and the Family*, **50**, 197-207.

Gurland, B. (1981) The borderlands of dementia. In *Clinical Aspects of Alzheimer's Disease, Ageing* (eds. N. Miller and G. Cohen), **15**, 61-80.

Gurland, B. Copeland, J., Kuriansky, J., Kelleher, M., Sharpe, L. and Dean, L.L., (1983) *The Mind and Mood of Ageing*, Croom Helm.

Hagnell, O., Lanke, J., Rorsman, B. and Ojesjo, L. (1981) Does the incidence of age psychoses increase? *Neuropsychobiology*, **7**, 201-11.

Ham, R. (1988) Speeding up discharge, *Health Service Journal*, **14** April, p.423.

Harrison, S., Martin, E., Rous, S. and Wilson, S. (1985)

Assessing the needs of the elderly using unsolicited visits by health visitors. *J. Roy. Soc. Med.*, **78**, (7), 557-561.

Harwin, B. (1973) Psychiatric morbidity among the physically impaired elderly in the community: a preliminary report. In *Roots of Evaluation* (eds. J. K. Wing and H. Hafner), OUP.

Hasegawa, K., Homma, A., and Imai, Y. (1986) An epidemiological study of age-related dementia in the community. *I.J. Geriatric Psychiatry*, **1**, 45-55.

Health Advisory Service (1982) *The Rising Tide: Developing Services for Mental Illness in Old Age*.

Helgason, L. (1977) Psychiatric services and mental illness in Iceland. *Acta Psychiatrica Scandinavica*, Suppl. 268.

Helgason, T. (1973) Epidemiology of mental disorder in Iceland: a geriatric follow-up.*Excerpta Medical International Congress Series*, **274**, 350-57.

Henderson, A.S. (1986) The epidemiology of Alzheimer's disease. *British Medical Bulletin*, **42**, (1), 3-10.

Henderson, A.S. and Huppert, F.A. (1984) The problem of mild dementia. *Psychological Medicine*, **14**, 5-11.

Henderson, A.S. and Jorm, A.F (1987) Is case-ascertainment of Alzheimer's disease in field surveys practicable? *Psychological Medicine*, **17**, 549-55.

Henderson, A.S. and Kay, D.W.K. (1984) The epidemiology of mental disorders in the aged. In *Handbook of Studies on Psychiatry and Old Age* (eds. D.W.K. Kay and G.D. Burrows), Elsevier pp.53-88.

Henneman, L., Du Toit, L., Patel, Y. and Ayling, E. (1987) *Tell them thank you very much : The first year of the Courtenay Scheme*, Exeter Health Authority.

Heston, L.L. (1984) Down's Syndrome and Alzheimer's Dementia: defining an association, *Psychological Development*, **4**, 287-94,

Heston, L.L., Mastri, A.R., Anderson, E. and White J. (1981) Dementia of the Alzheimer's type: clinical geriatrics, natural history and associated conditions. *Archives of General Psychiatry*, **38**, 1085-90.

Holzer, C.E.III, Tischler, G.L., Leaf, P.J. and Myers, J.K. (1984) An epidemiologic assessment of cognitive impairment in a community population. *Community and Mental Health*, **4**, 3-32.

Horrocks, P. (1986) The components of a comprehensive district health service for elderly people: a personal view. *Age and Ageing*, **15**, 321-42.

Huang, L-F., Cartwright, W.S. and Hu, T-W. (1988) The economic cost of senile dementia in the United States, 1985. *Public Health Reports*, **103**, (1), 3-7.

Hunter, D. (1987) Playing with numbers, *Health Services Journal*, 12 November, 1321.

Hunter, D., Burley, L., Headland, L. and Killeen, J. (eds) (1987)

Dementia: Developing Innovative Services in the Community,
Scottish Action on Dementia.
Ineichen, B. (1987) Measuring the rising tide: How many
dementia cases will there by by 2001? *B.J. Psychiatry*, **150**,
193-200.
Ineichen, B. (in preparation) How many part III residents are
mentally ill?
Jacques, A. and Burley, L. (1987) Strengthening the primary team
in support of dementia sufferers. *Geriatric Medicine*, **17**, (11),
15-16.
Jolley, D. (1981) Misfits in need of care. In *Health Care of the
Elderly* (ed.T. Arie), Croom Helm, pp.71-88.
Jolley, D., Smith, P., Billington, L., Ainsworth, D., Ring, D.
(1982) Developing a psychogeriatric service. In *Establishing a
Geriatric Service* (ed. D. Coakley), Croom Helm, pp.149-165.
Jorm, A.F. (1987) *Understanding Senile Dementia*, Croom Helm.
Jorm, A.F. and Henderson, A.S. (1985) Possible improvements to
the diagnostic criteria for dementia in DSM-III. *B. J.
Psychiatry*, **147**, 394-9.
Kahan, J., Kemp, B., Staples, F.R. and Brummel-Smith, K. (1985)
Decreasing the burden in families caring for a relative with a
dementing illness: a controlled study. *J. A. Geriatrics Society*,
33, 664-70.
Kay, D.W.K., Beamish, P. and Roth, M. (1964) Old age mental
disorders in Newcastle upon Tyne Part I, A study of Prevalence
Part II. A study of possible social and medical causes. *B.J.
Psychiatry*, **110**, 146-58; 668-82.
Kay, D.W.K., Foster, E.M., McKechnie, A.A. and Roth, M. (1970)
Mental illness and hospital usage in the elderly: a random sample
followed up. *Comprehensive Psychiatry*, **11**, 26-35.
Kay, D.W.K. and Bergmann, K. (1980) Epidemiology of mental
disorders among the aged in the community. In *Handbook of Mental
Health and Aging* (eds. J.E. Birren and R. B. Sloane), Prentice-
Hall, pp.34-56.
Kay, D.W.K., Henderson, A.S., Scott, R., Wilson, J., Rickwood, D.
and Grayson, D.A. (1985) Dementia and depression among the
elderly in Hobart. *Psychological Medicine*, **15**, (4), 771-88.
King, D. and Court, M. (1984) A sense of scale. *Health and
Social Services Journal*, 21 June, 734-5.
Kyle, D.R., Drummond, M.F. and White, D.M.D. (1987) The Hereford
District Department of Mental Health of the Elderly: a
preliminary evaluation. *Community Medicine*, **9**, (1), 35-46.
La Fontaine, J. (1987) Keeping the elderly in the community,
Health Service Journal, 26 February, p.245.
Leat, D. (1983) *A Home From Home*, Age Concern Research Unit.
Leff, J. (1986) Planning a community psychiatric service: from

theory to practice. In *The Provision of Mental Health Services in Britain: the way ahead* (eds. G. Wilkinson and H. Freeman), Gaskell, pp.49-60.

Leng, N. (1987) Help for home carers of elderly. *Health Service Journal*, 12 November, p.1320.

Levin, E., Sinclair, I. and Gorbach, P. (1983) *Supporters of Confused Elderly People at Home, extract from main report*; National Institute for Social Work Research Unit.

Levy, R. and Post, F. (1982) *The Psychiatry of Late Life*, Blackwell.

Lilof, V. (1983) Keeping them out of hospital. *Nursing Mirror*, 30 November, 36-8.

Lindesay, J. (1987) Dementia in 2001 (letter). *B.J. Psychiatry* 150, (5) 712.

Little, A., Hemsley, D., Bergmann, K., Volans, J., Levy, R. (1987) Comparison of the sensitivity of three instruments for the detection of cognitive decline in elderly living at home. *B.J. Psychiatry*, 150, 808-14.

Lodge, B. (1986) A model service based on needs. *Health and Social Service Journal*, 30 January, 144-5.

Mann, A.H., Graham, N. and Ashby, D. (1984) Institutional care of the elderly: a comparison of the cities of New York, London, and Mannheim. *Social Psychiatry*, 19, 97-102.

Maule, M., Milne J.S. and Williamson, J. (1984) Mental illness and physical health in older people. *Age and Ageing*, 13, 349-56.

May, D., McKeganey, N. and Flood, M. (1986) Extra hands or extra problems? *Nursing Times*, 3 September, 35-8.

McGrother, C.W., Castleden, C.M., Duffin, H. and Clarke, M. (1986) Provision of services of incontinent elderly people at home. *J. Epidemiology and Community Health*, 40, 134-8.

McGrother, C.W., Castleden, C.M., Duffin, H. and Clarke, M. (1987) Do the elderly need better incontinence services? *Community Medicine*, 9, (1), 62-7.

McKechnie, A. A. and Corser, C. M. (1984) The role of psychogeriatric assessment units in a comprehensive psychiatric service. *Health Bulletin*, 42, (1), 25-35.

McPherson, B. (1987) The success of a unique scheme for elderly mentally ill people. *Social Work Today*, 16 November, 18-19.

Meacher, M. (1972) *Taken For a Ride*, Longmans.

Moore, L. (1985) Elderly mentally infirm people: supportive relatives. *Community Care*, 14 November, 21-2.

Morgan, K., Dallosso, H.M., Arie, T., Byrne, E.J., Jones, R. and Waite, J. (1987) Mental health and psychological well-being among the old and very old living at home, *B.J. Psychiatry*, 150, 801-7.

MORI (1979) *Mental Illness: Public and Business Attitudes.*

Mortimer, J.A. (1983) Alzheimer's disease and senile dementia. Prevalence and incidence. In *Alzheimer's Disease* (ed. B. Reisberg), Free Press, 141-8.

Murphy, E. (1982) The social origins of depression in old age. *British Journal of Psychiatry*, **141**, 135-42.

Murphy, E. (1985) The GP and the psychogeriatrician. *Geriatric Medicine*, **15**, (5), 1.

Mushet, G. (1985) Coping with chronic dementia. *Health and Social Services Journal*, **45**, 4978, 12 December, 1576-7.

Nilsson, L.V. (1983) Prevalence of mental disorders in a 70 year-old urban sample: a cohort comparison. *J. Clinical and Experimental Gerontology*, **5**, (2), 101-20.

Norman, A. (1982) *Mental Illness in Old Age : Meeting the Challenge*, Centre for Policy on Ageing.

Norman, A. (1987) *Severe Dementia: The provision of long stay care*, Centre for Policy on Ageing.

O'Connor, D.W., Pollitt, P.A., Hyde, J.B., Brook, C.P.B., Reiss, B.B. and Roth, M. (1988) Do general practitioners miss dementia in elderly patients? *Br. M. J.* 197, 1107-10.

Parsons, P. L. (1965) The mental health of Swansea's old folk. *B. J. Prev. Soc. Med.*, **19**, 43.

Peace, S. M. (1980) *Caring from Day to Day*, MIND.

Peace, S. M. (1982) Review of day hospitals provision in psychogeriatrics. *Health Trends*, **14**, 92-5.

Persson, G. (1980) Prevalence of mental disorders in a 70 year old urban population. *Acta Psychiatrica Scandinavica*, **62**, 119-39.

Pfeffer, R.I., Afifi, A.A. and Chance, J.M. (1987) Prevalence of Alzheimer's disease in a retirement community. *A. J. Epidemiology*, **125**, (3), 420.

Philp, I. and Young, J. (1988a) An audit of a primary care team's knowledge of the existence of symptomatic demented elderly. *Health Bulletin*, **46**, (2), 93-7.

Philp, I. and Young, J. (1988b) Audit of support given to lay carers of the demented elderly by a primary health care team. *J. Roy. College of Gen. Practitioners*, **38**, 153-5.

Pinessi, L., Rainero, I., Asteggiano, G., Ferrero, P. Tarrenzi, L. and Bergomasco, B. (1984) Primary dementias: epidemiological and sociomedical aspects. *Italian J. Neurological Sciences*,5, 51.

Post, F. (1983) Psychogeriatrics as a speciality. In *Mental Illness: Changes and Trends* (ed.P. Bean), Wiley 279-95.

Power, M. and Kelly, S. (1981) Evaluating domiciliary care of the very old: possibilities and problems. In *Evaluating Research in Social Care* (eds. E. M. Goldberg and N. Connelly), Heinemann 214-34.

Preston, G.A.N. (1986) Dementia in elderly adults: Prevalence and institutionalisation. *J. Gerontology*, **41**,(2), 261-7.

Rabins, P. V. (1986) Establishing Alzheimer's disease units in nursing homes: pros and cons *Hospital and Community Psychiatry*, **37**, (2), 120-21.

Riccio, M. and Thompson, C. (1987) AIDS and dementia. *B.J. Hospital Medicine*, July, p.11.

Rice, A. (1984) Desperate in Seaford. *Community Care*, 13 September, 15-16.

Robertson, H. and Scott, D.J. (1985) Community psychiatric nursing: a survey of patients and problems. *J. Roy. Coll. of General Practitioners*, **35**, 130-2.

Rorsman, B., Hagnell, O. and Lanke J. (1985) Prevalence of age psychosis and mortality among age psychotics in the Lundby study. *Neuropsychobiology*, **13**, 167-72.

Rosen, G. (1968) *Madness in Society*, Routledge and Kegan Paul.

Rosenvinge, H. and Dawson, J. (1986) Sitting service for the elderly confused: part of an integrated programme of management. *Health Trends*, **18**, 47.

Roth, M. (1955) The natural history of mental disorder in old age. *J. Mental Science*, **101**, 281-301.

Roth, M. (1985) Some strategies for facing the problems of senile dementia and related disorders in the next decade, *Danish Medical Bulletin* 32, Alzheimer's Disease, Gerontology Special Supplement Series 1, 92-111.

Roth, M., Tym, E., Mountjoy, C.Q., Huppert, F.A., Hendrie, H., Verma, S. and Goddard, R. (1986) CAMDEX: a standardised instrument for the diagnosis of mental disorder in the elderly with special reference to the early detection of dementia. *B.J. Psychiatry*,**149**, 689-709.

Rowlings, C. (1981) *Social work with elderly people.* Allen and Unwin.

Royal College of Physicians (1982) Organic Mental Impairment of the elderly. Implications for research, education and the provision of services. *J. Roy. College Physicians of London*, **15**, 3-29.

Sayce, L. (1987) Revolution under review.*Health Service Journal* 26 November, 1378-9.

Schoenberg, B.S. Anderson, D.W. and Haerer, A.F. (1985) Severe dementia: prevalence and clinical features in a biracial U.S. population. *Archives of Neurology*, **42**, 740-43.

Scull, A. S. (1979) *Museums of Madness*, Allen Lane.

Serby, M., Chou, J. C-Y. and Fransen, E.H. (1987) Dementia in American-Chinese Nursing Home Population. *A.J. Psychiatry*, **144**, (6), 811-12.

Sheppard, M. (1985) Communication between GPs and an SSD. *B. J. Social Work*, **15**, 25-42.

Shibayama, H., Kasahara, Y., Kobayashi, H. *et al.* (1986)

Prevalence of dementia in a Japanese elderly population. *Acta Psychiatrica Scandinavica*, **74**, 144-51.

Shinfuku, N., Sugita, T., Shingai, N. (1984) Presenile and senile dementia in Japan. *Asian Medical Journal*, **27**, 392-9.

Shulman, K. (1981) Service innovations in geriatric psychiatry. In *Health Care of the Elderly* (ed. T. Arie), Croom Helm.

Simons, H. R. (1982) Voluntary day centres for the mentally infirm. *Geriatric Medicine*, **12**, (3), 62-4.

Simpson, C. J. (1984) Doctors and nurses use of the word confused. *B. J. Psychiatry*, **145**, (4), 441-3.

Sinclair, I. (1988) Residential care for elderly people. In *Residential Care: The Research Reviewed* (ed. G. Wagner), National Institute for Social Work/HMSO.

Smith, C.W., Staley, C.J., and Arie, T. (1986) Admission of demented old people to psychiatric units: an assessment of recent trends. *Br. Med. J.*, **292**, (6522), 15 March, 731.

Smith, G.and Cantley, C. (1985) *Assessing Health Care: a study in organisation evaluation*, Open Press.

Smith, N.K.G. (1988) Continence Advisory Services in England. *Health Trends*, **20**, 22-3.

Smith, T. (1984) Brendoncare: an initiative in the care of the elderly. *Br. Med. J.*, 289, 909-10.

Smyer, M. A. and Gatz, M. (eds) (1983) *Mental Health and Ageing: Programs and Evaluations*, Sage, Beverly Hills.

Srole, L., Langer, T.S., Michael, S.T., Opler, M.K. and Rennie, T.A.C. (1961) *Mental Health in the Metropolis*, McGraw-Hill.

Sternberg, E. and Gawrilova, S. (1978) Uber Klinisch-epidemiolog-ische untersuchungen in der Sowjetischen Altenpsychiatric. *Nervenarzt*, **49**, 347-53.

Stilwell, J. A. *et al.* (1984) Changing demands made by senile dementia on the NHS. *J. Epidemiology and Community Health*, **38**, 131-3.

Sulkava, R., Wikstrom, J., Aromaa A. *et al.* (1985) Prevalence of severe dementia in Finland. *Neurology*, **35**, 1025-29.

Tym, E. (1989) Diagnostic assessment. In *Dementia Disorders: Advances and Prospects* (ed. C. E. Katona), Chapman and Hall.

Vetter, N. J., Jones, D.A. and Victor, C.R. (1984) Effect of health visitors working with elderly patients in general practice: a randomised controlled trial, *Br. Med. J.*, **288**, 369-72.

Volans, J. (1989) Psychological approaches. In *Dementia Disorders: Advances and Prospects* (ed. C. E. Katona), Chapman and Hall.

Wattis, J. P. (1988a) Geographical variation in the provision of psychiatric services for old people, *Age and Ageing*, **17**, (3), 171-80.

Wattis, J. P. (1988b) Senior Registrar training in old age psychiatry in the United Kingdom. *Bulletin of the Royal College of Psychiatrists*, **12**, 233-4.

Weiler, P.G., Mungas, D. and Pomerantz, S. (1988) AIDS as a cause of dementia in the elderly, *J. American Geriatrics Society*, **36**, 139-41.

Weissman, M. *et al* (1985) Psychiatric disorders (DSM- III) and cognitive impairment among the elderly in a U.S. Urban community. *Acta Psychiatrica Scandinavica*, **71**, 366-79.

Wertheimer, A., Ineichen, B. and Bosanquet, N. (1985) *Planning for a Change*, Campaign for Mentally Handicapped People.

Weyerer, S. (1983) Mental disorders among the elderly: True prevalence and use of medical services. *Archives of Gerontology and Geriatrics*, **2**, 11-22.

Whitehead, A. (1976) The prediction of outcome in elderly psychiatric patients, *Psychological Medicine*, **6**, 467-79.

Whitehead, A. (1981) A single-ward approach to the elderly mentally ill. *Health Trends*, **13**, 99-100.

Whitehead, A. (1983) Mental infirmity: the cottage hospital approach. *Geriatric Medicine*, February.

Whittick, J. E. (1988) Dementia and mental handicap: Emotional distress in carers. *B.J. Clinical Psychology*, **27**, 167-72.

Wilkin, D. and Hughes, B. (1987) Residential care of elderly people: The consumers' views. *Ageing and Society*, **7**, 175-201.

Wilkin, D. and Williams, E. I. (1986) Patterns of care for the elderly in general practice.*J. R. Coll. G.P.s*, **36**, 567-70.

Wilkin, D., Durie, A., Wade, G., Jolley, D. and Stout, I. (1984) *Specialist Services for the Elderly: A study of referrals in geriatric, psychiatric and social services*, University Hospital of South Manchester.

Williamson, J., Stokoe, I.H., Gray, S., Fisher, M., Smith, A., McGhee, A. and Stephenson, E. (1964) Old people at home: their unreported needs. *Lancet*, i, 1117-20.

Wimo, A. (1988) Personal communication.

World Health Organisation (1986) *Dementia in Later Life; Research and Action*, Technical Report Series 730.

INDEX